GW01375037

Newnham, our Newnham

Newnham, our Newnham

Nigel Bell

First Edition Published 2025

ISBN: 978-1-916722-38-5

Unless otherwise stated, all photographs have been taken by the author or members of his family, with the exception of Figs. 25, 29 and 30, whose provenance it has not been possible to trace. Other illustration sources are acknowledged in the text.

For permission requests, please contact the author at nnbx2@hotmail.com

Supported by Hampshire Archives Trust and Newnham 900

Designed by Tim Underwood
Printed by Sarsen Press, 22 Hyde Street, Winchester

Front cover:
Aerial photograph of Newnham, reproduced by kind permission of Mick Murnaghan
Back cover:
Photograph of Naish's Farm and pond, with Tithe Barn in the background, early twentieth century

CONTENTS

FOREWORD

by the Right Reverend David Williams, former Bishop of Basingstoke

For 900 years St Nicholas' Church, Newnham, has stood as a testimony to the presence and love of God in this wonderful and ever-changing village community.

Countless generations of people have worshipped in this ancient church, bringing their joys and sorrows and hopes and fears before God. Children have been baptised, couples united in marriage, and loved ones laid to rest, in the conviction that the God who created all things is interested in and cares for the day-to-day details of our lives.

We give thanks for 900 years of worship in this place and look forward, with hope and trust in the God who sustains His church, to its ongoing and fruitful ministry. May it continue to be a blessing to the village, the benefice and further afield. As Christians we rejoice in our history and step forward with confidence into our future.

So, in the light of these 900 years of testimony, I commend Nigel Bell's book on the history of Newnham, which arises from his deep commitment to the local community and also from his regular worship at St Nicholas' Church.

INTRODUCTION AND ACKNOWLEDGEMENTS

My grandfather, W. M. C. Pechell, came to live in Newnham in 1890. He made enquiries of those already here, often from families which had lived locally for several generations, about the village and the church. He also studied the Parish's church registers (births, deaths and marriages) and built up a body of information about the location. I inherited his documented research and data, which I have tried to add to over the past 50 or so years. Under the circumstances, it has seemed a pity not to record what I know, or what I *think* I know, about the village in this volume produced to commemorate the building of St Nicholas' church 900 years ago. In addition, I have added data from other people's research (which I hope I have duly acknowledged). Furthermore, I have included some of the speculations which I have developed in the light of these studies. Of course, *speculations* can only be *speculations*, and the point of recording them is to offer ideas for others to explore.

Newnham is presently a small village of some 90 dwellings, the core of which was established many centuries ago. It is what it is today because of what its current inhabitants and those in the past have made it. From time to time, changes brought by external pressures or transient visitors have altered the landscape or influenced our community. Because the name 'Newnham' is of Anglo-Saxon derivation, it seems appropriate to consider what may have happened or, in some cases, definitely happened, since that time, and that period can be considered as a baseline. Exactly when Newnham was first settled, we do not know because there are no written records, e.g. Anglo-Saxon charters. However, the village has features that give clues to something of its earliest years, from which we can make deductions about its past.

This study, *Newnham, our Newnham*, does not set out to be an academic work, although I have provided references to other documents or research which relate to our community. It aims to bring together a range of aspects about Newnham's past (and sometimes present) which have not been addressed in other studies of the neighbourhood: for example, Newnham's origins and later history (Chapter 1); its roads and footpaths (Chapter 2); local farming practice and how it has changed (Chapter 4); local industries (Chapter 5); and a study of Newnham's church and churchyard (Chapter 7). The volume also includes some account of Newnham's older houses (Chapter 8), and information about services (e.g. mains water) provided by third parties (Chapter 10). The Appendices include reproductions of maps featuring Newnham and the surrounding area between the fourteenth and nineteenth centuries, data examining the effects of the Black Death on local populations, and conclude with a survey of flora and fauna in Newnham over eight decades, based on a lifetime of personal observation.

The standard scholarly reference work about all aspects of Hampshire is *A History of the County of Hampshire*, published by Victoria County History (VCH) in five volumes between 1900 and 1913.[1] I refer regularly to VCH in the chapters which follow. The original publication is in the process of being revised and, when complete, it is expected to cover all the villages and towns of the county.[2]

In summary, through many centuries, Newnham has continued, sometimes suffering setbacks, and sometimes thriving. The composition of the village has altered, as circumstances have altered: and in the past 70 years change here has accelerated. Nevertheless, Newnham, *our* Newnham has persisted as the home for our evolving community. It is up to us to ensure that any changes which are proposed, and which take place, will meet our needs and those of

1 William Page (ed.), *A History of the County of Hampshire* (Victoria County History), particularly Vol. 4 (1911).

2 An updated VCH study of Newnham, Nately Scures and Up Nately has been under way for some years and publication is expected soon. The VCH revision for communities in the Basingstoke area is ongoing: a VCH 'short', *Mapledurwell*, was published in 2015, followed by *Steventon* (2016), *Mediaeval Basingstoke* (2017) and two others.

the next several generations. Importantly, any future changes should not put at risk those valued finite features – buildings and other important structures, or wildlife habitats – which have survived. These always seem to be under threat, especially from those who are not aware of Newnham's background.

Newnham, our Newnham is dedicated to all our forebears in the village whose contributions we take for granted, and to all those who succeed us in the hope they will aim to retain Newnham's free spirit.

There are many people who have helped to bring this study to fruition. I should like to place on record my gratitude to the Right Reverend David Williams, former Bishop of Basingstoke, for contributing the Foreword, in one of his last acts before leaving to take up his new position as Bishop of Truro. My thanks are due to the Friends of St Nicholas, Newnham, for their help in getting the book launched. The Newnham 900 Committee has been enthusiastic in its support, and I am grateful to Al Richmond for locating the aerial photograph which graces the front cover and is also reproduced on page 71. I thank the photographer, Mick Murnaghan, for his kind permission to reproduce it, as well as the originators of other photographs (where known) and copyright owners, who are acknowledged at the appropriate places in the text. My family has provided much sterling support, from chauffeuring and photography to proofreading.

Finally, I would like to put on record my indebtedness to Kate Richards for her very skilful editing of all that follows; without her careful review of the earlier drafts, lots of errors would have remained and much helpful cross-referencing would have been omitted. Nevertheless, for any omissions or inaccuracies I am to blame.

CHAPTER 1

NEWNHAM'S ORIGINS AND LATER HISTORY

Timeframe

Before the first written reference to Newnham, we cannot be confident about the surrounding area in which the village is set. Two Neolithic flint hand axes have been found: one at Naish's Farm, one between Newnham Lane and Compfield Copse; and other ancient finds have been recorded.[1] There is no proof, either way, that the land was being farmed by the Celts before the Roman era, or whether the Romans were involved in economic activity here. Roman evidence from neighbouring communities, e.g. North Warnborough, Hook, Mapledurwell and Old Basing[2], suggests the local area was probably peopled, but whether Newnham itself was occupied is uncertain. There are no Roman-derived place names nearer than Silchester (*Calleva Atrebatum*), which lies about 12 miles north-west. Once the Romans had withdrawn in 410 AD there followed a long period during which the whole country became politically disturbed; it was a time of warfare during which the Saxons and other incomers (Angles, Frisians, Jutes) occupied different parts of Britain. During this time farming is likely to have suffered and perhaps it was neglected locally. Once

1 *Hampshire Treasures Survey*, Vol. 2 (Basingstoke and Deane) (Hampshire County Council, 1979), p. 201.

2 There was an extensive Roman villa near Lodge Farm, North Warnborough; Roman tiles have been found in Hook behind the White Hart; the route of the Roman road discovered in 1949 from Chichester (Sussex) to Silchester ran just west of Mapledurwell; there is also anecdotal evidence that about the 1960s or 1970s, Roman remains were briefly uncovered at a farm to the west of Old Basing, but there is no further information.

fields are no longer managed for agriculture they rapidly revert to woodland.[3] Over the ensuing three or four centuries any local fields which had once been cleared, but were subsequently uncultivated, could have reverted to woodland.

Two areas in North-East Hampshire were originally known as forests: the Forest of Eversley and Pamber Forest. These were not forests in the sense of jungle, but in the sense of much woodland with pasture and arable, set aside for the preservation of big game that could be hunted by royalty. That said, there may well have been impassable areas, particularly valley bottoms before they were drained. In such places wetland thickets could have been found – fallen trees with willow and alder predominating, combined with sedges, reeds and other water-tolerant species. Some mediaeval valley floors *may* have been like the illustration (**Fig. 1**). Within these forests, there are today many villages with names which indicate that in Saxon times, the area was well-wooded. When a place name ends in 'ley' or 'ly' it implies a woodland clearing. A list of such place-names includes Riseley, Eversley, Mattingley, Hazeley, Hartley (Wespall, Wintney), Bartley (Heath on Hook Common), Nately (Scures), Bramley and Tadley. These villages are ranged around Newnham.[4]

The name Newnham is of Anglo-Saxon derivation, meaning the new 'ham' or new settlement. As so often in this part of England, there is a dearth of very early (e.g. Anglo-Saxon) written records to tell us about our own community or about our neighbours. The Anglo-Saxon Chronicle is the first relevant document which records a battle between the Anglo-Saxons and the Danes at Reading in 871. The Anglo-Saxons lost and withdrew to the south. There was a further battle soon after at Basing[5], which they also lost. These are the earliest two references to Reading and Basing, but there is no reference to anywhere locally, e.g. Newnham, nor are there any local, relevant Anglo-Saxon charters. It has been

3 When a cultivated field or open grassland is untended for ten or more years, it becomes colonised by scrub and trees, initially by bramble, hawthorn and birch, soon after by ash, maple and oak trees, which soon grow to 30 feet or more.

4 There are other villages nearby, which indicate that many fields had already been cleared for arable, and these may not have reverted to woodland, such as Stratfield (Mortimer, Saye and Turgis), Winchfield and Dogmersfield. These clearances may date from pre-Saxon times to make fields for growing food to feed the Roman colony.

5 The Anglo-Saxon Chronicle for 871 states that 'King Aethelred and Alfred his brother, led great levies there to Reading and fought against the host [...] And the Danes had possession of the place of slaughter. [...] And a fortnight later king Aethelred and Alfred, his brother, fought against the host at Basing, and there the Danes won the victory.' *The Anglo-Saxon Chronicle* (Everyman's Library No. 624), translated and introduced by G. N. Garmonsway (J. M. Dent & Sons Ltd, 1953), p. 70.

suggested by Richard Coates[6] that Newnham dates from 'mid-Saxon times', i.e. *c.* AD 700–750. It is appropriate to mention here that some toponymists believe 'ham' names indicate early settlement by Anglo-Saxons.[7] If this is correct, it reinforces the view that Newnham existed by the early eighth century.

The fact that the core of the village seems to have been structured around the village green (i.e. not a linear village such as Rotherwick, and not a dispersed settlement like Winchfield) indicates it could have been an early Anglo-Saxon community: '[*it may be that*] villages possessing greens tend to be the earliest in their particular regions, that they go back in general to what might be called "frontier days".'[8] The original purpose of The Green may have been to provide an enclosed area to protect the villagers' livestock from raiders or wild animals, such as wolves.[9]

Inevitably, due to lack of documentation, the exact date when the new 'ham' was established is conjectural, and the reason for its establishment is equally conjectural. It seems reasonable to accept that Newnham was separated as a new community, somewhere around AD 700. Because it is situated round a village green, The Green may have been the site where livestock were corralled each evening; there is also the possibility (although this hypothesis has not been explored by excavation) that the Lord of the Manor settled the newcomers around a green because he aimed to position it as a regular market or fair at the intersection of roads leading north, south, east and west.

To avoid any misunderstanding, it is proper to record here that Newnham and Mapledurwell have often been linked in the past, particularly since 1086, so it has been suggested[10] that it may have been population pressure in Mapledurwell in Saxon times, which led to Newnham's establishment. However,

6 Richard Coates, *The Place-Names of Hampshire* (Batsford Ltd, 1989), pp. 122–123.

7 See Margaret Gelling, *The Place-Names of Berkshire*, Part 3 (English Place-Name Society, Cambridge, 1976), Vol. 51, p. 816 *et seq.* Also: Eilert Ekwall, *The Concise Oxford Dictionary of English Place-Names*, 4th edn (Oxford: Clarendon Press, 1960), Introduction, pp. xiv–xv.

8 W. G. Hoskins & L. Dudley Stamp, *The Common Lands of England and Wales*, Collins New Naturalist series No. 45 (Collins, 1969), p. 32.

9 Wolves were becoming rarer in mediaeval times, and are thought to have become extinct in England in the early sixteenth century (Wikipedia).

10 'The Manor Farm at Newnham is on a raised patch of Lower Bagshot Sand in the surrounding clay. [...] there is a clear suggestion [...] that this was a settlement in more marginal land under pressure of population growth.' R. Coates, *op. cit.* I find this an unconvincing argument because this 'marginal land' extends to no more than perhaps 20 acres (8 hectares). It is hard to imagine it proving satisfactory for a new settlement. (Nigel Bell).

it is also appropriate to query whether in the pre-Norman period Newnham was necessarily part of Mapledurwell manor[11], or whether it may have been included in the land-holding of a different manor.

The earliest written record

At the time of the Domesday Survey[12], there is no mention of Newnham, which at that date is generally believed to have been part of Hubert de Port's Manor of Mapledurwell.[13] At that date Hugh de Port (thought to be a close kinsman) 'held 55 Lordships of the King in Hampshire, whereof Basing was one which became Head of the Barony'.[14] His other local holdings from the King were, *inter alia*, Bramshill, Chineham, Heckfield, Kempshott, Nately Scures, Oakley, Sherborne St John, Stratfield Turgis and Upton Grey, and from Bishop Odo[15], besides others, he held Monk Sherborne and Wootton St Lawrence.

Hugh de Port died and was succeeded by his son, Henry. Early in the twelfth century Henry founded a Priory in West Sherborne as a dependency of the Benedictine abbey of St Vigor, in Normandy. The foundation cannot be dated with any great precision, but it is likely to have been about 1127 (see Chapter 6, Pamber Priory and St Nicholas' Church). In the foundation charter, he gave Newnham's church and tithes to the Priory. This is the first written record of the village.

Newnham's Setting

The origins of Newnham and the possible dateline for its creation have been discussed. It is now time to consider its location. The Anglo-Saxon Chronicle

11 Manor: an estate held by a landlord from the king which could embrace more than one parish.

12 Domesday Survey of 1086 (a.k.a. The Domesday Book, sometimes shortened to Domesday).

13 William Page (ed.), *A History of the County of Hampshire* (Victoria County History, 1911), Vol. 4, p. 149 'comprising within its boundaries [...] Mapledurwell, Newnham and Up Nately, together with Andwell.'

14 William Dugdale, *The Baronage of England*, Tome I, 1675, p. 463. See Appendix 3, Church Documents (1).

15 Bishop Odo of Bayeux was William the Conqueror's half-brother and was given estates in England which Hugh de Port managed.

records the two battles in 871, at Reading, and Basing (footnote 5). Basing is some 12 miles south of the centre of Reading, and the Danes must have pursued the Saxons, although the route each army used seems not to have been conclusively researched. If at that time the Loddon-Lyde valley was largely undrained, perhaps swampy and perhaps impassable for militias of whatever size, these two armies may have followed the route from Reading, along the ridge, which connects through Heckfield, Mattingley and Rotherwick to Newnham, then round the higher ground above Mapledurwell and on to Basing. The site of the battle itself is said to be Basingfield, at the southern end of Old Basing. Alternatively, the armies may have marched west of the river Loddon to reach Basing. None of these lesser communities are mentioned in the context of either battle; the Chronicle itself is always very economical in its use of words to summarise its annual reports. However, it seems likely these settlements already existed.

Our written source of early data about communities near Newnham is the Domesday Survey of 1086. From this and other data, it is evident that the following villages, with their earliest recorded dates, existed: Hartley Wespall (1086); Mapledurwell (1086); Mattingley (1086); Nately Scures (1086) and Odiham (1086)[16]; Rotherwick (about 1100); Heckfield (1194); Hartley Wintney (1270) and Hook (1236).[17] [18] There is little doubt that if these communities merited a mention at their various dates, they will already have been long established. The implication is that there must already have been a network of local tracks or roads connecting these villages. Furthermore, Newnham was effectively the village on a crossroads: on a route from Reading (following higher ground) via Riseley, Heckfield, Mattingley and Rotherwick towards the south via Odiham to Farnham (894) and Fareham (1086)[19], and from the west (e.g. Basing and Basingstoke) and towards the east and eventually to London.

There are no early maps to give us any guide about local commercial routes, but it must be assumed that traders who had a surplus of (say) horses, cattle, sheep, pigs or other livestock, and hides, wool or cheese, would have taken them

16 These dates are quoted from E. Ekwall, *op. cit.*

17 The Hook reference is to '*boscus de Hoc*', perhaps alluding to extensive woodland north of the current community.

18 These dates are from R. Coates, *op. cit.*

19 Ekwall, *op. cit.*

to some regular market. Evidently, Newnham could have been well placed for regular or occasional product exchange.

Topography

The core of Newnham stands round The Green on the ridge that stretches northwards to Rotherwick/Mattingley and southwards to Butterwood/Greywell; to the east, the land falls away fairly gently (with slight undulations) to Hook and then the River Whitewater. Coming from the west, the land rises steeply from the valley to the top of the hill, with the highest point (St Nicholas' church and Manor Farm) 312 feet or 97 m above the datum. In fact, these two buildings are sited where one can get long views westward over the Loddon and Lyde rivers.

It seems unusual that the community should have been established on the top of a hill away from water, because the nearest permanent stream, the Lyde, is well down the hill and about 1,000 yards distant. Normally it would be a long way to carry domestic water supplies. However, our forebears realised that it was possible to dig wells on the top of the hill and be confident of always finding water apart from in exceptionally dry years.[20] The explanation seems to be that the surface layer of soil on Newnham Green consists of plateau gravel which sits on layers of clay – this clay prevents the water from draining away; further away from The Green the soil is semi-permeable clay, London clay, which in turn rests on another clay layer that is impermeable. It seems the rain soaks through the upper layers but can then go no further: when a well is sunk, water is almost always found near the surface.

Concerning what is actually known about existing roads in southern England, the earliest map is the Gough map (*c.*1325–1350), illustrated in Appendix 1 (Map 1). From this it is evident that there was no major road anywhere near Newnham. To the south, the main road to the far south-west went from London via Guildford, Farnham, Alton and Winchester, then to Salisbury and on to Exeter (approximately the current A3, A31, A30). To the north, the road to Bristol went from London, close to Windsor, then Reading,

20 In the very dry year of 1976, the owner of Railway Cottage, Newnham Road (Mr Frederick Fulker) assured me that his well – which lay about 50 yards from a very steep railway cutting – still held water within ten feet of the surface.

Hungerford, Marlborough and on to Bristol (essentially the current A4). Although Basingstoke is shown on the map, it clearly does not feature as a place of major significance.

Glimpses of history

What is known from the Anglo-Saxon Chronicle has been discussed above. If the two armies came through Newnham, one would guess that the few inhabitants concealed themselves as best they could, in local woodland, until the warriors had passed. And if there were other warring bands during the ensuing decades and centuries, concealment was probably the best strategy. During the reigns of many English kings there were often long periods of peacefulness, but not a great deal is known about what was happening hereabouts. For example, there is no evidence about the ebb and flow of military activity during the Wars of the Roses, or any of the other insurrections which occurred from time to time.

We do have small glimpses of local problems from the Basingstoke rolls recording Views of Frankpledge, a sort of Manor Court which was held regularly to receive reports from a tithing-man, or his substitute, about the state of the various villages in the Basingstoke Hundred. In 1427 John Fereby, Rector of Newnham, who had assaulted Thomas Stukeley with a staff and had drawn blood, was fined 6d.[21] In 1461 John Stukeley was fined 12d, 'because he made the ford badly in the common road, at Newnham, in Wildmore [*allowing the river to run into the meadow of Wildmore*]' and also fined a further 12d 'because the gate leading to Wildmore is broken and badly fastened'.[22] Again in 1470, 'John Stukeley was fined 3d for not repairing the gate towards Wildmore.'[23] John Stukeley was the Lord of the Manor and does not seem to have taken much notice of the Court. In 1583 William Whitcombe[24] was fined 10s for not coming to be sworn in at the Court as tithing-man[25], and in 1587, James

21 F. J. Baigent & J. E. Millard, *A History of the Ancient Town and Manor of Basingstoke* (London: Simpkin, Marshall, 1889), p. 261.

22 *Ibid*, p. 286.

23 *Ibid*, p. 303.

24 William Whitcombe died in 1586, and his inventory (Hampshire Record Office AO/79) shows that he must have been a successful mixed farmer.

25 Baigent & Millard, *Basingstoke*, p. 348.

Turner was fined 3s 4d, for 'breaking the pound at Newnham and taking out two horses'.[26] There were other such infringements brought to the attention of the Court but none of them were of much consequence.

However, there was a major disruption to life during the First English Civil War, between 1642 and 1646. No major battles were fought in Newnham's immediate locality, but there were serious battles at Alton in December 1643 and at Cheriton in March 1644, both of which resulted in victories for the Parliamentarians over the Royalists. These and other military incidents were presumably accompanied by groups of soldiery moving about the countryside, and it is not unlikely that Newnham saw a share of these movements. Indeed, there may have been some kind of fight in the local fields because a pistol ball has been found by metal detectorists. Perhaps of most significance for the village was the prolonged siege of Basing House, four miles from Newnham, between 1643 and 1645: the Marquess of Winchester held Basing House for the King against the Parliamentarians who were led initially by Sir William Waller; then finally, in October 1645, Oliver Cromwell succeeded in breaking down the House's fortifications. There is a local tradition that the Barracks at the southern edge of the village may have accommodated soldiers at this period, but no documentary evidence has been traced.

There are other glimpses: for example, in 1601 Queen Elizabeth I came to visit Basing House and it is almost certain that she passed through Newnham. There must have been many another royal person who came this way between London and the West Country; however, we do not have a record. In 1666, the plague appears to have struck Basingstoke with great severity[27] and it is likely that Newnham also suffered, but again there are no relevant registers. As recorded in Chapter 2, from about 1400 until 1786 the main road to the West Country (the Great West Road) passed through the middle of Newnham, and we can be sure there was regular movement of all sorts of travellers through the village. We can also be sure that when there were national outbreaks of diseases, the village will have experienced them.

What impact the French Revolutionary and Napoleonic Wars (between 1793 and 1815) had on Newnham is uncertain. Perhaps villagers were called up for military or naval duties, but there is no record. However, the threat from

26 *Ibid*, p. 351.

27 *Ibid*, p.105.

the French in the late eighteenth and early nineteenth centuries (a perpetual distraction for the English) clearly made itself felt in so far as the Great West Road was rerouted from Newnham Road and Crown Lane to what is now the A30 over Scures Hill by 1786. This will undoubtedly have had some impact on the economy around The Green, and after some time it caused the Crown Inn to be closed and the business to be moved on to Hook Common where the Hogget (formerly the Dorchester Arms) now stands.

Perhaps the next important event so far as Newnham is concerned was WW1. How the war affected Newnham is unclear. At the time, most of Hook was also included in Newnham parish. Evidently many able-bodied men from Hook, Nately Scures and Newnham village were called up for service in the Army and Navy. Like so many others from around the country, they died fighting the Germans. There is a tablet to their memory in St Nicholas' church, Newnham, and one serviceman, Sgt Morris, was laid to rest near the lychgate. Evidently there was a fear that German spies or sympathisers might try to damage local infrastructure and so a detachment of troops could be found at Hook station, and a further guard is known to have been posted at the railway bridge on Crown Lane (**Fig. 2**). After WW1, a war memorial was set up at the junction of the A30 and Newnham Road, on Jubilee Green, Hook, at the point where Newnham, Hook and Nately Scures meet.

All too soon after WW1 ended in 1918, the threat of a new war turned into reality: WW2 began on 3 September 1939. Although Newnham, as a village, was much less affected than some other communities, nevertheless all able-bodied men aged between 18 and 41 were called up for National Service in the Army, Royal Navy or Royal Air Force, as were the majority of single women who were called upon to undertake duties in support of the British forces. One of these was Joan Chapman, née Harbert, who told me that she worked for Lansing Bagnall, Basingstoke, applying phosphorescent paint to compasses used by the night-flying RAF.

During the run-up to the war, measures were taken to prepare for the risk of invasion by the Germans. Three pill-boxes were built: one on Newnham Road (**Fig. 3**), one at the top of Crown Lane between the entrance to Manor Farm and the corner of the churchyard – this has since been removed – and one about 150 yards north of Lyde Mill, Newnham Lane, on the river and facing west. The Crown Lane pill-box faced down the hill and there were large cylinders of concrete that were to be pulled into the road so as to delay the enemy vehicles and to give British troops or perhaps the LDV (Local Defence Volunteers – later the Home Guard) enough time to destroy them. The pill-box on Newnham Road was also provided with similar delaying concrete blocks and in addition, at the top of the railway cutting, there were mini-pyramids of concrete to prevent the enemy getting past the defence. Additionally, at various strategic points two- or three-man trenches were dug where the LDV could hide while firing on any enemy: one was at the crossroads on Newnham Green. Like everywhere else in Britain, Newnham residents were subject to rationing – meat, butter, cheese and several other food items, also clothes or other fabrics, and petrol. As a result of the latter rationing, there were very, very few cars on the roads and bicycling was much safer than it is today.

From time to time there were air raids by German bombers. The warning siren would go and sometimes it was necessary to take shelter. On one occasion, I (aged nine or ten) was running with my lunch to the air raid shelter when I saw overhead a Heinkel 111 bomber flying towards Nately Scures; fortunately, no bomb was dropped. However, there was a very sad occasion in 1940: on the morning of 18 August 1940 a detachment of a Royal Engineers bomb disposal unit arrived at Newnham. Two bombs had been dropped on the railway embankment west of the bridge on Crown Lane. One exploded and caused damage to windows and ceilings all round the village. The other did not explode and needed to be defused quickly as it was a threat to the main line. The REs knew they were in danger and as they were digging down, the bomb exploded, killing six engineers. Their NCO, Lance-Sergeant Button, was thrown through the air by the blast, but survived. Dennis Gary, who lived in 2 Crown Cottage, Crown Lane, recalled: 'We suffered a lot of damage to our homes. And a great six-foot girder came through the roof of my granddad's house and the bedroom ceilings were down – and not repaired until after the war because of the lack of materials. My brother Norman and I were playing in the garden when it happened and we can both still remember the awful shower of body parts that fell all around the area. Those brave men are now remembered on a plaque in Newnham church, at Hook Station, and a memorial at the railway bridge.'[28]

Although these Royal Engineers are commemorated at St Nicholas' church,

28 Extracted from *The Villager* (the monthly parish magazine for the communities of Newnham, Nately Scures, Mapledurwell and Up Nately), November 2023.

Newnham, they were buried at Aldershot. There is a grave in Newnham churchyard, near the steps to Crown Lane, where Private Marriner is buried; and on the north side of the church lies the body of Second Lieutenant James Alexander Macintosh, aged 24, whose family lived in Hook. To the best of my knowledge no service personnel from Newnham itself died during WW2.

Since WW2, a major impact on Newnham has been the coming of the M3 motorway, in 1971, with junction 5 about two miles distant. This has made it very easy for residents to drive to London or Southampton and all the various intermediate employment centres; and also to Heathrow, Gatwick and Eastleigh airports. Then, after the village was put onto main drains (see Chapter 10), 'old' Newnham, with houses around The Green occupied by cottagers who rented them (and who often had local roots), steadily disappeared. Nowadays these same dwellings belong to owner-occupiers.

CHAPTER 2

NEWNHAM'S ROADS AND FOOTPATHS

The development of communications with communities away from Newnham has been reviewed in Chapter 1, Newnham's Origins and Later History. In that chapter it was shown that the main English road networks passed well away from this part of North-East Hampshire, as demonstrated in the Gough map of *c.*1325–50 (Appendix 1, Map 1). The aim of this chapter is primarily to discuss the roads and footpaths relating to the original parish of Newnham. Nevertheless, it seems more rounded to consider the roads and footpaths in the whole civil parish, in view of the fact that the civil parish of Newnham now also comprises part of the original parish of Nately Scures.

Roads

Tylney Lane[1]

Tylney Lane is the road that leads from Newnham Green past the Old House at Home pub and, currently, towards Tylney Park golf course and Rotherwick parish. In the past it has also been called Park Lane and Beehive Farm Lane, or just Beehive Lane.

1 For the record, it is referred to as Tylney Lane in the national census returns of 1881 and 1901.

When one walks that route these days it seems to be too narrow a track to have been a main route, and so it is. Being mystified, I decided about 1980 to study the hedges on both flanks and found that the western side seemed to have a larger number of plant species compared with the eastern side, which suggested the hedges were of different date.[2] Then I noticed beyond the roadside hedge, to the east, there was another hedge demarcating the field, and this proved to have about the same number of species as the hedge on the west. The conclusion is that the original roadway was bounded by these two outer hedges, west and east, which are about 66 feet or 20 m apart – a distance that had been normal for old roads. Presumably, when Tylney Lane was tarmacked, or perhaps merely metalled, the landowner arranged for bushes and trees to be planted between the newly demarcated road and the field to the east. I suggest that, at least by 1774[3] and possibly much earlier, we can be confident that Tylney Lane was an important route connecting Newnham and Rotherwick.

At the Rotherwick end, the roadway has become no more than a footpath, although it clearly was once a bridleway. In the 1950s and 1960s there were two teachers at Hook School, the Misses Bellamy, who used to ride their horses along Tylney Lane and on to Rotherwick. I spoke to one of them (the other was dead) towards the end of her life and she confirmed this fact. And Mrs Jenny Gibbons, who was brought up at **Beehive Farm** (see page 14), told me that as a girl, she could remember riders passing the house. I believe that after WW2, the farmer who occupied that land, Alan Davis, disliked horses crossing the fields which he was cultivating. Although he was himself a good horseman, he seems to have arranged for riders to be excluded from the fields. I cannot vouch for this, but it is what I have heard. Probably, when the golf club was created in 1974, the management arranged for any bridleway status to be discouraged, and they seem reluctant to allow the footpath to continue across the golf greens; walkers are encouraged to walk round the club's boundary with Tylney Hall Hotel. I believe that originally the footpath also went directly over the Rotherwick playing field and emerged on Stroud Green Lane. At some point it

2 Hedgerow dating is a simple technique that can give a rough idea of the date of a hedge. One takes a series of 30-metre sections along a hedgerow and counts how many different woody species (bushes, climbers or trees) are in each section, then one averages the result. Each species counts for a century. So, if one finds an average of three species in a hedge, it is 300 years old +/- 200 years. It is a useful tool but rather imprecise.

3 The date when the Tylney estate map was made (Hampshire Record Office 10M48). See Appendix 1, Map 6.

was diverted to the current concrete path which joins the northern drive into Tylney Park Golf Club.

The date when Tylney Lane was called Park Lane is unclear, but the road was so identified on some Ordnance Survey maps. However, in my lifetime it has been called Tylney Lane and that identification was agreed by Newnham Parish Council about 1980. The road has also been called Beehive Farm Lane after the name of the now derelict farm which is reached about 250 yards into Rotherwick parish, on the western side of the footpath. Sadly, at the time of writing the farmhouse is no more than two chimney stacks and a heap of rubble (**Fig.** 7). In WW2, the land was occupied by Mr and Mrs Edward Morris, who lived at **Newnham Corner**. There is a neglected, and now dilapidated, building to be seen on the west of the footpath just over the parish boundary where Mrs Morris (Marion) milked two or three cows; she could be found wheeling a small churn on her bicycle round the village, and doling out milk to householders who brought her their own jugs. I do not know when she stopped this business: Edward Morris died in 1945, and she may have died soon after.

Ridge Lane

As mentioned above, the 1774 map also shows Ridge Lane. Currently, Ridge Lane leaves Newnham crossroads towards Rotherwick, but the unusual aspect is that it does not follow any ridge. In fact, after the original southern gates to Tylney Hall, it drops down and follows a fairly low-level road to the bottom of Post Horn Hill, where it turns left, and climbs steeply up to the top end of Rotherwick Street. In that parish, the lane is called Post Horn Lane, and the tradition is that when coaches were climbing or descending that part of the road, they blew a horn to warn others on the road of their arrival. Perhaps carters and others in charge of wide vehicles also made the same signal, but history does not relate.

Many years ago, when speaking to the Hampshire County archaeologist, Philip Colborn, I learnt that in his view it was possible that the land to the west of Post Horn Hill had originally been part of the common land of Rotherwick village. However, the Lord of the Manor rerouted Ridge Lane, because it would have gone undesirably close to his new house, the first Tylney Hall. This may be correct, because the route from the southern gate to Tylney Hall, at the Newnham end, does follow a ridge straight to the gateway at the northern end. It would certainly have been a more direct route between the two villages.

Crown Lane

This lane is so called because it led up from the lower lying land of Nately Scures into the village of Newnham and at the top on the left, it passed the Crown Inn; the building today is called Crown Lodge. The age of this house is unclear, but its style suggests it might be seventeenth century[4], although it has clearly been added to and altered at intervals since its foundation. It must have been a considerable pleasure for chapmen, carters, livestock drovers and other travellers to breast the hill and find a source of refreshment awaiting them, particularly as their animals could find water from ponds on The Green and presumably graze, while their owners rested. As an aside, I believe that often one will find there used to be an alehouse or an inn on the roadside as one entered a village, just as one will often find a similar hostelry closely adjacent to where roads cross rivers.[5]

To my mind, the remarkable fact about this roadway is that from about 1400[6] it used to be one section of the Great West Road[7], and Crown Lane was still on this main route as late as 1783; that is to say, it was *the* main road from London via Basingstoke, Andover and Salisbury to Exeter. Soon after 1783, the road was straightened to follow the track of the A30 through Nately Scures, and down Scures Hill: this had happened by 1786.[8] It seems the French were again threatening England, and the government chose to improve this road to make it easier for guns and other ordnance to travel rapidly from London to the South Coast or *vice versa*. However, it is also very clear that Crown Lane itself is very ancient. For the last 150 yards, as the lane rises up to the village, it is a hollow way: the road surface currently lies six to ten feet lower than ground level on

4 Houses dating from the sixteenth and seventeenth centuries were typically constructed round a central chimney stack. Eighteenth- and nineteenth-century dwellings were usually, as it were, 'hung' between chimney stacks at each end.

5 Examples of the latter are the pub (formerly the Red Lion) at Water End beside the Lyde on the A30, the Crooked Billet beside the River Whitewater in Hook, the White Lion beside the River Hart in Hartley Wintney, and many more.

6 The main road from London to Land's End, as can be seen on the Gough map of *c.*1325–1350 (Appendix 1, Map 1), went from London via Guildford, to Farnham, Alton, Winchester, Salisbury, Shaftesbury and Exeter. Perhaps by 1377, based on economic evidence, Winchester was becoming by-passed and a new main road was developed from Salisbury via Andover to Basingstoke and thence through Newnham to Bagshot and Staines and on to London. See C. Cochrane, *The Lost Roads of Wessex* (New York: Augustus Kelley, 1969), pp. 34 and 37.

7 For an example, Newnham is clearly shown in John Ogilby's *Britannia* (1675) in the roadmap section from London to Andover (see Appendix 1, Map 4).

8 Daniel Paterson, *A New and Accurate Description of All the Direct and Principal Crossroads in Great Britain* (London: T. M. Longman, 1796), p. 27.

each side (**Fig. 4**). This is the result of the surface of the road being loosened and worn down by the passing traffic over the centuries, and the surface then being eroded downhill by the rain. The soil here is heavy clay and probably the villagers over the centuries, putting down whatever road building material was to hand, could not stabilise the surface and so it wore away. Perhaps it was in this defile on the steeper part of the hill that highwaymen operated. There were three cases in the eighteenth century when these miscreants were caught and the matter was reported in the press[9], but there may have been other instances of such criminal behaviour where the offender was not detained. Perhaps more examples will come to light with more research.

I did try to hedge-date the boundaries of this road, but the work was inconclusive. This was partly because the hedges were worn and neglected, and I believe the line of the road may have been changed slightly when the railway bridge was built and the railway embankment created, about 1838.

To the south of the bridge, and about 200 yards towards the A30, the old main road branched north towards the River Lyde, the track now called Green Lane (Newnham Footpath/Bridle path No. 6) reaching the current main road, just to the east of the Water End Mobile Home Park. Of course, all of this area is in Nately Scures, and in the *Survey of the Manor of Nately Scures*, dated 1561[10], it is clear that if the road had any local appellations it would usually have been described as the King's Highway.

About 1900 a brickyard, Hook Brick & Tile Company, was opened immediately below the railway bridge. It obviously flourished for several decades and into WW2; a short siding existed to convey away the wire-cut bricks, and a goods train pulled into the works' siding regularly. There used to be six cottages for the workers within the brickyard and a manager's house that is still on Crown Lane. I believe there was a problem with the bricks in that there were small stones in the clay, and when the bricks were baked, the clay and the stones heated and cooled differentially. This could result in the bricks being unstable and cracking. After WW2 the competition from major brick makers, e.g. London Brick Company, is believed to have caused the brickyard to close about 1950. The site from where

9 *London Evening Post*, October 22, 1728; *Whitehall Evening Post,* November 28, 1747; *London Evening Post*, November 22, 1750. I am very grateful to Bob Clark, writing in the Victoria County History Newsletter No. 13 'Highwaymen', for this information.

10 *A Survey of the Manor of Nately Scures*, 1561 (Hampshire Record Office 21M58/E37).

the brick clay was dug stretches about 200 m (about an eighth of a mile) back from Crown Lane and when brick-making ceased the hollowed-out area was used, for many years, as a raw household garbage dump for some weeks each year while the former Chineham incinerator was closed for annual maintenance. At this time a great deal of unsuitable rubbish was also brought to this site, e.g. material like engine oil, half-empty paint drums, asbestos lagging. When, after about ten years, the landfill was complete the site was capped with clay. Thereafter a series of chemical reactions took place underground, and on wet days, it was possible to see bubbles rising from the surface, presumably methane or other gases. Then about the year 2000 it was noticed that the trout, and other indicator species of a healthy river, had gone from the Lyde. The Environment Agency traced the problem back to a ditch which fed into the river. This ditch originated immediately below the former rubbish dump, so that some kind of chemical 'soup' was reaching the river and either directly poisoning everything or depleting the oxygen in the water with a similar result. Remedial action had to be taken by Hampshire County Council and so far as we know the problem has been solved. However, whenever there has been continuous heavy rain, it is important to keep watch in case contaminated water once again escapes from a manhole cover below the bridge, flows along the lane and eventually reaches the Lyde.

An earlier brickyard, Newnham Brick Works (a.k.a. Musselwhite's yard), was opened around the late 1870s and was still operating in 1935. This brickyard lay about 200 m (an eighth of a mile) further along Crown Lane towards the A30, technically within Nately Scures parish. Currently it is an overgrown wildlife area with little or no sign of its former industrial activity.

In August 1940, a German bomber dropped two bombs on the railway line about 200 m west of Crown Lane. This has been discussed in Chapter 1.

On a lighter note, there is a curious tale about Thomas Hutchins, the late Dennis Gary's grandfather, who worked in Musselwhite's brickyard and lived close by with his in-laws in **Crown Cottages**. One evening after a thirsty day's work he went down to the Red Lion (a.k.a. the Iron Bull) at Water End to get a pint or two. He left for home while it was still light and he felt nicely cooled until he turned into Crown Lane, where he experienced a strangeness. He tried to push himself forward: he could see his home, but he couldn't get there. It wasn't long before he knew what the strangeness was – between him and his home stood 'the lady in black'. Thomas was frozen to the spot and couldn't believe what he saw. He turned about and walked as fast as he could, out of Crown Lane, up Scures Hill and down through the brick fields again. It seems 'the lady in black' may have been the daughter of a former Rector of Nately Scures who had died in a dogcart accident, or that she was a Mrs Bunbury. She was said to frequent Crown Lane, but not everybody saw her, and she used to appear at the most unusual times.

It may be of interest that when climbing Crown Lane, on the right-hand side just as the steepest part of the hill begins, there are some steps flanked by brickwork. Apparently in the 1920s, W. M. C. Pechell of Newnham Hill did not care for the Rector of Newnham, so he had the steps constructed to enable him to walk each Sunday to St Swithun's, Nately Scures; meanwhile the rest of his family went to St Nicholas' church.

Newnham Road

Pursuing the theme of the former Great West Road: at the crossroads on Newnham Green the main road (Crown Lane) turned right into Newnham Road[11], leading to Hook (which until 1932[12] was mostly in Newnham parish) and then on to Hartley Row, Bagshot, Brent and eventually London. (As an aside, it may be worth mentioning that Camberley only grew and expanded as a community after 1802 with the establishment of Sandhurst Royal Military College.) The first part of Newnham Road was evidently a drift way, funnel-shaped with the narrow end on The Green and widening out on to Hook Common. Once it reached the Common, somewhere close to the start of Morris Street, the main road turned left, while a branch (perhaps in Saxon times the more important part of the road) carried on over the Common to Odiham. The earliest Newnham estate map made about 1700[13] shows this funnel shape quite clearly and it is still traceable on more recent Ordnance Survey maps[14] because the hedge boundaries of the fields on either side of the road are quite clear. After

11 See footnotes 6 and 7.

12 Before 1882, Hook had been partitioned between Newnham, Nately Scures and Odiham. In that year the parish boundaries were realigned so that Nately Scures stretched no further east than Old School Road, and Odiham came no further north than part of Hook Common. In 1932, Hook was separated from Newnham and made into a separate parish. This was almost inevitable because after Hook railway station was opened in 1883, the village began to grow steadily.

13 Hampshire Record Office 33M71. Part of this map is shown in Appendix 1, Map 5.

14 See Appendix 1, Maps 7 and 8.

about 1950, when more ribbon development on the eastern side of the road began, the field boundary to the east of the road became subsumed into the gardens of the various dwellings. An interesting feature on the earlier maps is the village pound. The site still survives, and the wooden post and rail fence could still be seen in the 1940s. It is possibly of some significance that about 10 yards to the south of the pound is a large oak tree, possibly planted about 1750, which may have been placed to provide shade for any livestock that had been detained there.[15] In 1982, I did a hedge-dating exercise along the west or south-west field boundary from Newnham Green to Railway Cottage. Clearly this is an old hedge, judging by the girth of some of the trees that were growing, not only the well-established oaks, but some field maples and bullaces, and also in one or two places there were ancient woodland indicator species like bracken, bluebell, goldilocks buttercup and pignut. There may be *less* significance in these latter plants, but they could be long surviving vestiges of woodland that was cleared very many centuries ago. The outcome of my study, based on the woody plants alone, suggests that this hedge could be 900 to 1,100 years old, and could date from about AD 900 or earlier.

For the sake of completeness, it is appropriate to recall that when the Act for Repairing the Road from Hertford Bridge Hill to the Town of Basingstoke was passed in 1737, the preamble stated that it had 'become so ruinous and bad, that many parts thereof, in the winter season, are impassable to coaches'. Turnpikes were erected and those using the road paid a tariff as laid down in the Act. The Act does not specify where the turnpikes were placed and there is no tradition of one along Crown Lane or Newnham Road, but there may have been one near the Red Lion pub on the Lyde. There is a house opening onto Water End Lane, called Turnpike House, but it was built much later than 1737. One of the features of these turnpike roads was the regular erection of milestones, and there used to be one on Newnham Road, almost opposite the old village pound, stating 41 miles to Hyde Park Corner.

After the railway was constructed in 1838, Newnham Road, which used to turn east where Morris Street begins, was straightened so that currently it runs on the north side of the railway cutting. At this time a new field-side hedge was established and it is likely the plants used were, as far as possible, those of

15 There is a similarly placed old oak directly to the south of the pound at Nately Scures, which lies just off the A30 on the west of Heather Row Lane.

some former hedge which was lost when the cutting was constructed. Certainly, hedge-dating suggests that this hedge may be older than 1838, because of the average number of different woody species to be found (four, which suggests the hedge could be 400 years old). Before the railway was constructed, the line of the track was surveyed, and compensation was paid to various landowners. This line survey revealed a previously unknown alehouse, the Traveller's Rest, which stood a little to the south of where Newnham Road turns sharply east at the railway fence. In pre-railway days, there seems to have been a bridge on the Common immediately south of the railway, shown in the 1561 *Survey of the Manor of Nately Scures* (see footnote 10) as 'Hackingryth bridge', and on the Langford map of 1616 (Appendix 1, Map 3) the area is identified as Hackingrow. There is a major tributary of Newnham Brook that rises on Hook Common south of the A30 and flows down beside Old School Road; when it reaches the railway, it is channelled into a large pipe or culvert[16] that flows under the bridge and re-emerges between two houses, **Kedron** and **Oak Hanger**. Presumably this railway bridge is called Kingsbridge because the name derives from a corruption of these sixteenth- and seventeenth-century names.

Newnham Lane

Like Crown Lane, Newnham Lane also shows signs of being very old. As one leaves The Green, one begins a steep descent down towards the River Lyde and this is also a hollow way (**Fig. 5**), not quite as deeply cleft as Crown Lane, possibly because for several centuries it did not carry as much traffic and consequently eroded less. It has one remarkable feature, its name. It is puzzling to know why a lane leading from Newnham – a relatively small village compared with Old Basing – should be identified with Newnham rather than Old Basing, or at least 'Basing'. Basing, from its name the 'settlement of Basa's people', is of Anglo-Saxon origin (see Chapter 1, footnote 5). It would be logical to assume that it had more substance by the time that Newnham, the 'new settlement', became established. One wonders whether Newnham, because of its crossroads position, was seen to be a significant place 'with potential'.

Probably the most important building along Newnham Lane, within our village, is **Lyde Mill**, converted into a private house about 1960, I believe, by

16 Apparently in the 1930s and 1940s local boys would crawl through this pipe as a dare.

Denys Oppé.[17] As regards the mill's history, there is no certainty when the first building was founded, but it has been proposed that it 'probably marks the site of one of the two mills comprised in Mapledurwell in 1086'.[18] Mills were vital elements in village life in mediaeval times because villagers would carry to them their own sacks of corn for grinding into flour so that they could make their own bread. When it was a working mill, it was powered by two breast-shot waterwheels with wooden paddles (still in position outside the building).[19] When it ceased to function as a mill is uncertain. The Lyde used to be forded at this point as just to the south of the bridge, the slope down to the stream is evident, and the road was slightly realigned when the bridge was made. The coping bricks of this bridge are very similar to the bridge at the bottom of Pyotts Hill, Old Basing, which was opened in 1826.[20] Perhaps both bridges are roughly contemporaneous.

Blackstocks Lane

A document of 1561[21] seems to identify that the lowest section of Crown Lane, and part of Blackstocks Lane, was then called Nether Way; it also indicates there was an area of land called Blackstocks that may have lain alongside this road. The derivation is uncertain: however, the word 'stock' can mean a tree trunk, or perhaps the butt of a felled tree that has not yet rotted away. If this is the origin in this case, I suggest that at some time – possibly two or three centuries before 1561 – the location referred to was woodland that had been cleared leaving the stumps, and the name was retained.

Andwell Lane

This runs alongside the Lyde and part-way along the edge of Andwell Priory Farm. Only the section of road nearest the A30 is within Nately Scures. The Priory ceased to exist in the fourteenth century when it was handed over to Winchester College. The name Andwell has an Anglo-Saxon origin, meaning 'duck stream'.

17 The Oppé family lived in and owned Manor Farm, Newnham including ownership of the mill.

18 William Page (ed.), *A History of the County of Hampshire* (Victoria County History, 1911), Vol. 4, p. 157a.

19 Monica Ellis (ed.), *Water and Wind Mills in Hampshire and the Isle of Wight* (Southampton University Industrial Archaeology Group, 1978), p. 37.

20 Wikipedia.

21 *A Survey of the Manor of Nately Scures* (*op. cit.*). Translated from the Latin by G. W. Willis.

Water End Lane

The lane starts at the Iron Bull (a.k.a. the Red Lion) on the A30 and leads north-west under the railway bridge to Gold's Farm, and thence to Newnham Lane. It forms the parish boundary with Old Basing, as far as the railway.

The A30

For completeness, it seems appropriate to mention this road also, which was first classified as an 'A' road by its present number by the Ministry of Transport in 1921. In 1561 (see footnote 21) it was described as a 'footpath' which ran between the many Baredown closes: i.e. the fields on either side of the path over what must then have been an open hillside. In no way was it then a road because, as already described, the main road from Basingstoke to London followed Green Lane (footpath No. 6 mentioned below) to Crown Lane and Newnham Road. But, as already explained, the road was straightened for military reasons between 1783 and 1786 to follow the present line.

Footpaths

To make the most of this section, it would be helpful to consult either the Newnham Footpath map or to use the Ordnance Survey Explorer map No. 144 (Basingstoke, Alton & Whitchurch, Odiham, Overton & Hook; scale 1:25,000). With the latter, it should be possible to follow which footpath is being described.

The centre of Newnham is poorly provided with footpaths; there are effectively only two, one of which, as has been discussed already, starts as a road, Tylney Lane. However, a little away from the centre, it is easy to access several which in turn join up with a network of others, leading to the various neighbouring communities. These various footpaths are as follows:

Church Path

Currently this is the footpath, known officially as Newnham Footpath No. 3, which is most used by parishioners and visitors from Hook and elsewhere. Its origin lies in the fact that a large swathe of Hook was, until 1932, part of the parish of Newnham (see footnote 12). St Nicholas' church was the focus of community life and religion from at least 1125. The present church certainly existed in 1127, and in mediaeval times people were regular churchgoers for the good of their souls and for the major landmarks in life, e.g. marriage and the baptism of children, then death and burial. We can be reasonably sure that Church Path is at least 900 years old. This footpath would have been created to provide access for people from Hook to get to church, being manifestly much shorter than the high road, with a better walking surface. In early days and until the turnpike roads were developed, public roads, particularly in winter, were often deeply rutted and almost impassable through heavy clay. At the Newnham end, on The Green, the path was carefully built up and its remains are visible to this day. How far Church Path's surface improvement was extended, so that the path was less wet underfoot, is now unknown, but originally it may have been made good the whole way between both parts of the settlement. *En passant,* a detailed study of Church Path has been made by the Friends of Church Path and is available at **https://bit.ly/4jmaruL**.

Footpath No. 1

This begins on the north side of Newnham Lane to Old Basing, about 400 m (a quarter of a mile) from the edge of The Green. After about 350 m, it reaches the parish boundary and becomes Rotherwick FP 1 leading to Stroud Green and on to Summerstead Farm, Hartley Wespall and Sherfield on Loddon. It seems possible that this was the route, closest to the Lyde River, which was usually above the floodplain and perennially passable in the centuries before the river valley was drained. If this is a correct interpretation, the track may have continued to the south side of Newnham Lane, through Webb's Copse and thence southward following the contour. Perhaps this is one of the oldest footpaths here, but it will require much further research, including work with metal detectors and perhaps excavation to prove or disprove the theory. An earlier name for this pathway was Lone Barn Lane, because there was a building – presumably a barn – standing on the western side of the track. It still existed when the Newnham Tithe Map of 1842 (Appendix 1, Map 7) was prepared. The name 'Lone Barn' still appears on the Ordnance Survey map (scale 1:2,500) of 1939 and may yet be in the map-maker's lectionary. However, the barn is long gone. At some point in the past, it seems that a former landowner had arranged for the track to be planted with shrubs, e.g. hazel and hawthorn, so that it could only be negotiated with difficulty. It is unclear why this should have happened, but it may have been because the landowner was trying to create a pheasant cover. In winter 1975, Newnham villagers and others, such as the Ramblers, the Scouts and children from local schools, came together for many weekends to remove the obstructions; the footpath is now clear.

Footpath No. 2

Some 250 m along FP No. 1, north of Newnham Lane, a footpath branches west down to the Lyde and a footbridge crosses the stream. The path continues as Old Basing FP No. 10. Whether or not this is an old pathway is unclear and its purpose may have been to enable labourers to reach the farms where they were employed on either side of the river. But on the Newnham side, which is hedged on both flanks, its primary purpose in recent years has been to reach the adjacent fields. However, it can be argued that livestock may have been driven down to the river to quench their thirst or, in the more distant past when the land beside the river was probably marshy, cattle may have been driven there to summer graze.[22] In 1976 a new footbridge was built over the Lyde by the Old Basing Scouts; it was opened at Easter in the same year by the local MP, David Mitchell (**Fig. 6**).

Footpath No. 4

Technically this is a Nately Scures footpath, which connected The Barracks to what is now the A30. It was, presumably, a path to enable workers to get to their employment. It passes between **Cromwells** and **The Holdings**, and has in the past been the subject of much argument; however, there can be no doubt that it is an authorised Public Right of Way, of long-standing.

Footpath No. 5

This is a short path southward from the A30 at the top of Scures Hill; it soon joins footpath 719 (see below).

22 This thought is prompted by the existence of the farm named Summerstead to the north, adjacent to the Lyde. A stead or steading is a farm building and the implication is that in the distant past, in summer it was the base for someone supervising livestock that were grazing on the edge of Wildmoor: perhaps comparable to the way some Swiss still drive their cattle each summer to the uplands, the Alpage, to graze the alpine pasture, thereby preserving their lowland meadows for winter hay production.

Footpath No. 6

Also called Green Lane, this used to be part of the Great West Road and is mentioned under Crown Lane above. It is classified as a BOAT (Byway Open to All Traffic) and may currently give an insight into what roads would have been like before the turnpikes when their surfaces were cut up by carts and carriages.

Footpath No. 7 *(both of them)*

This path has been slightly re-routed: previously it used to go through St Swithun's churchyard towards **Painter's Pightle** and **The Old Rectory**; today the authorised path goes along the track to the church. The late Dennis Gary told me that in about 1937, he had gone down on a late summer evening to take refreshment to his grandfather Thomas Hutchins, who was the church sexton at St Swithun's. Just imagine the scene: Harry King, who lived at **Painter's Pightle** along Blackstocks Lane, had been in the Red Lion (the Iron Bull) for a jug or two, and as darkness was falling he set off home along the footpath that used to pass through the churchyard. Meanwhile, Thomas Hutchins, in his white shirt, had been digging a grave. Having reached the statutory six feet he stopped and, as the light was fading, he began to climb his ladder to the surface. This spectre appeared just as Harry King arrived; with a cry of horror he fled, leaping the stile in one, and raced home deeply shaken. Thomas laughed his head off.

Footpath No. 8

This is Coop Lane, connecting Andwell Lane with Blackstocks Lane and forms the parish boundary with Mapledurwell. The derivation of 'Coop' is unclear; in 1561, it was called the Upper Way (see footnote 10).

Footpath No. 9

A short path from Coop Lane to reach Blackstocks Lane between **Painter's Pightle** and **The Old Rectory**. It would have enabled farm workers from Nately Scures to reach Andwell Priory Farm by joining Mapledurwell footpath No. 29, which runs through Mill Wood.

Footpath No. 10 *(suppressed)*

Regrettably, this footpath no longer exists. It used to connect the western end of the unadopted road into the Barracks down to Crown Lane. Whether or not it was designed *solely* to enable those living in the brickyard cottages to reach Hook, or those at the top of the hill to walk down to the brickyard for work is now unclear. However, it seems that once the brickyard had ceased to function, about 1950, the owner of the intermediate land succeeded in having this footpath suppressed by Hampshire County Council. This was a serious mistake by the County because it was a very valuable path facilitating a round-trip on foot, good for exercise and for dog-walkers.

Footpath No. 11

This used to be an unmade-up track from **The Hogget** (at the intersection of the A30 and the A287 on Hook Common) to Heather Row, but since the development of **Hollybush View** (on Hook Common), currently the location of Astral P.M.S. Ltd, it has been partly tarmacked.

Footpath No. 12

Technically, the footpath begins on the Old School Road, but in practice it starts just before the entrance to Foster's Business Park and cuts through the short piece of common land to reach the A30 almost opposite Heather Row Lane.

Footpath No. 717

This footpath and the other three in the 700 series used to be Greywell footpaths, and so remained after the M3 was built in 1970. In about 1990, Newnham Parish Council approached Greywell Parish Council with the suggestion that because these paths were now seldom used by Greywell people but were regularly used by Newnham people, the parish boundaries should be altered so that the M3 became the new joint boundary. The idea was accepted, and these footpaths are now part of Newnham's network. However, the County Council decided to retain the initial '7' in the series running from 717 to 735 so as to maintain an historic connection to Greywell. Footpath 717 connects Heather Row and Blackstocks Lane, running past Lower Cakesbridge Copse, Snipes Wood and Hang Wood and then alongside the M3.

Footpath No. 719

This connects footpath No. 717 past Upper Cakesbridge Copse and connects with footpath No. 5.

Footpath No. 720

This connects Heather Row and Blackstocks Lane and runs alongside the M3.

Footpath No. 735

A short footpath between Heather Row and the bridge over the motorway leading on to Butterwood and Up Nately, also Heather Lane and Klondike.

CHAPTER 3

NEWNHAM'S POPULATION

The following can only be an approximation. We do not have any true figures, either for the houses immediately round The Green or for how many families each may have contained, earlier than the census of 1841. The objective of this chapter is to give the reader some idea of the population on various arbitrary dates, based on the limited documentary evidence available.

Our earliest indication of Newnham's possible population comes from the Domesday Survey of 1086 when Newnham is believed to have been part of Mapledurwell.[1] At that date Mapledurwell consisted of two villeins, and 12 bordars and five slaves, 19 families in all.[2] Of these, it is perhaps not unreasonable to suggest there may have been seven families living around Newnham Green, the core of the village. It is appropriate to record here that demographers do not seem to have been able to agree what multiplier to use to convert these heads of families into probable population figures: one recent study[3] proposes 'a

1 Julian Munby (ed.), *Domesday Book: No. 4, Hampshire* (Chichester: Phillimore & Co. Ltd, 1982), p. 46b, c #24.

2 A villein was an unfree landholder of the Lord of the Manor, a bordar was similarly unfree and possessor of a smallholding, a slave or serf was effectively owned by the Lord of the Manor. See John Richardson, *The Local Historian's Encyclopedia*, 2nd edn (London: Historical Publications Ltd, 1993).

3 Quoted in Stephen Broadberry, Bruce M. S. Campbell and Bas van Leeuwen, 'English medieval population: Reconciling time series and cross-sectional evidence' (University of Warwick, part of the project 'Reconstructing the National Income of Britain and Holland, c. 1270/1500 to 1850', 2011), p. 4.

multiplier of 4.5 to 5.0' per household. I have assumed there were five persons per family; consequently, there were perhaps some 35 inhabitants in the village.

Similarly, there seems to be no agreement regarding what multiplier to use to show population growth in the Middle Ages. I have found figures varying between 1.0025% and 1.004% growth per year until about 1350. In 1348, and again in 1362, the Black Death or, as it was then known, the 'Great Pestilence', struck England.[4] During this period, local evidence indicates that about half of the population within 7½ miles of Newnham died. This figure is based on the Registers of the Bishop of Winchester, Bishop Edington[5], which recorded the dates when all the new clergy were inducted, village by village. During these Black Death years, there was a very unusual increase in the number of new inductions. It seems reasonable to suppose that usually at this time, whenever a new parson was inducted, his predecessor had died, and presumably the ordinary population died at a similar rate as the clergy. This explains the population drop in the table below. Newnham lost its Rector in 1349, but whether he died of the plague or from natural causes is unknown. On balance, it seems likely to have been the plague.

We can never know the exact population. The following figures are offered to give an estimate of what the numbers may have been:[6]

1086	35	
1100	36	
1200	46	
1300	59	
1348	67	(Black Death, which killed an estimated half of the local population.)
1351	33	
1360	34	

4 See Appendix 2 for a fuller examination of how the Black Death affected 30 local villages in the vicinity of Newnham.

5 Dom. S. F. Hickey (ed.), *The Register of William Edington, Bishop of Winchester 1346–1366* (2 vols., Hampshire Record Office for Hampshire County Council, 1986 Part 1 and 1987 Part 2).

6 I have used the following population growth factors to reach the relevant estimates: 1086–1348, 1.0025%; 1362–1500, 1.0004%; 1500–1801, 1.005%. After 1801 I think it probable that the population depended increasingly on incomers from elsewhere to supplement the local birth rate and to an extent people moving away for better-paid work.

1363	17[7]
1400	20
1500	29
1600	47
1700	78
1788	120[8]
1801	135
1841	164 (census)[9]
1861	160 (census)
1881	165 (census)
1901	229 (census)

7 An estimated further half of the remaining population may have died during the second wave of the Black Death.

8 In 1788, parish clergy were required to send information about the communities they served to the Bishop, including the size of the population. Newnham, which then included much of Hook, reportedly had 232 people. I have assumed that just over half lived in and around The Green. See W. R. Ward (ed.), *Parson and Parish in Eighteenth-Century Hampshire: Replies to Bishops' Visitations* (Hampshire County Council, 1995), p. 304.

9 For the purposes of this study, I have only used census data from houses round Newnham Green, Lyde Mill, and Newnham Road as far as the current boundary with Hook, and in addition – selectively – the Barracks. The aim is to have all the data restricted to the 'core' area.

CHAPTER 4

AGRICULTURE AND LOCAL FARMING PRACTICE

Like every other rural community in North-East Hampshire, the backbone of Newnham's economy in the earliest times was based on farming; there was no other local industry of scale. There were, as far as we know, two corn mills and somewhere (as yet unidentified) up to three fulling mills[1], but these were not major employers. There was no mining, no fishing, no manufacturing industry, no evidence of a major trading business: the focus of life was farming. Naturally, there were tradesmen with specialist skills, perhaps a blacksmith, perhaps a harness maker or wheelwright, all in support of farming; and there may have been a baker, a butcher or a cobbler. We can also be confident that there were ale houses because ale was a reasonably safe drink at a time when there were many water-borne diseases[2]: these cottage industries may have made their own malt, or somewhere nearby there may have been a maltster. Whether there was any establishment we would recognise as a pub is unclear; however, individual householders who made their own brew of ale and had a surplus may have signified the fact in some way[3] for thirsty customers to buy. Whatever

1 *A History of the County of Hampshire*, Vol. 4, ed. William Page (Victoria County History, 1911), p. 157a.

2 Tea only reached Britain around 1650, and coffee was introduced later in the seventeenth century (Google).

3 It may not be relevant to the rural Hampshire scene at that time, but in Nigeria when a housewife has surplus palm wine for sale, she signifies the fact by hanging a branch outside her house. (Author's personal knowledge.)

specialised skills individuals in the community possessed and marketed, they almost certainly were involved in some way in farming: either cultivating their own small plots or working for a more prosperous neighbour.

Initially, most of the farming here will have been small scale and may perhaps have taken place on strips of land held in common in the open fields. We know that in Mapledurwell this strip farming continued until 1796 when an Enclosure Act[4] rationalised the management of the land. The Tylney estate map of 1774[5] (Appendix 1, Map 6) also reveals strip farming west of the River Lyde.[6] However, there is no evidence one way or the other that Newnham ever had an open field system for villagers to farm and there is no information about land enclosure in the parish.[7] Unfortunately, if any information about farming or land holding in Newnham existed from Norman times, or earlier, it was presumably kept in the archives of the Lord of the Manor, and will have been lost when Basing House fell to Cromwell in 1645 and caught fire.

In Newnham, the first farming facts of which we can be certain come from Wills and Inventories in the sixteenth century. For example, Robert Preston (Rector of Newnham from 1521 to 1534) left three different people a calf each and, to his councillors (an unknown number), a lamb each, thus indicating he was farming his own glebe. From the other five sixteenth-century inventories, it is clear that many fields were of four or five acres; those farmers were growing wheat, oats, barley and peas and they had small milking herds of cattle (six to 12 cows), flocks of sheep (40 to 80), and usually some pigs and poultry. The sheep's wool seems to have been sold, but William Whitcomb[8] (died 1586) left 15 lbs of wool; he also had a spinning wheel. There are five Newnham inventories for the seventeenth century: an analysis suggests the farming pattern is largely unchanged except that only one farmer has sheep, and another farmer (whose family is known later to have been spinning wool) had bought in 11 fleeces. These inventories also reveal that four farmers owned yokes of oxen, which were

4 John Chapman & Sylvia Seeliger, *A Guide to Enclosure in Hampshire 1700–1900*, Hampshire Record Series Vol. XV (Hampshire County Council, 1997), p. 51.

5 Hampshire Record Office 10M48.

6 J. Chapman & S. Seeliger, *op. cit.*, p. 65. '50 acres (Wildmoor, a common pasture) recorded as open at the tithe commutation in 1842 (21M65/F7/199/1–2).'

7 *Ibid.*, p. 56. 'The tithe apportionment of 1840 (21M65/F7/168/1) appears to show all the land enclosed.'

8 Inventory, Hampshire Record Office AO/79.

clearly used for ploughing and harrowing before sowing cereals by hand. These farmers also owned horses which were presumably used for personal transport, and perhaps for hauling carts. Also of interest is the fact that three farmers seem to have been marketing cheese, butter, bacon and possibly diversifying into onions (one instance). *En passant*, the evidence from Newnham is, in general, confirmed from Wills and Inventories of farmers in Nately Scures. The database is small, but the evidence we have is of mixed farming on small fields producing a surplus of milk that was turned into cheese and butter, and sometimes flitches of bacon, for sale off the farm. How, and to whom, these sales were made is presently unknown. Nor do we know the sizes of any of these farms.

There is a vignette, drawn by Thomas Langdon and dated 1616 (Appendix 1, Map 3), regarding a seventeenth-century property of Corpus Christi College, Oxford, at what is now Owens Farm, Hook.[9] In this case, we have a modest insight into how about 130 acres in Newnham were split between two tenants: Christopher Lester, the College's local steward, and Hugh Matthews, both of whom had other holdings in Mapledurwell. The former had 67 acres at Owens Farm divided into ten fields or copses; Hugh Matthews held some 63 acres in eight fields or copses. From this it is clear that all the fields were relatively small, the largest being about 11 acres.[10] It is possible that these two farmers were working rather larger than average holdings.

There is a very incomplete picture shown in a badly worn Newnham map[11] of about 1700 held at the Hampshire Record Office, Winchester (Appendix 1, Map 5). Unfortunately, the schedule that went with it no longer seems to exist, and as a consequence it is not possible to state with any confidence which fields were tenanted by which farmer. Nevertheless, it is clear from the map that all the fields were comparable in size to those depicted in the Langdon map.

A much clearer picture emerges with the Tithe map (Map 7 in Appendix 1 dated 1842) and accompanying award (1840).[12] Fortunately, the 1841 census enables us to confirm the names of the various farmers. The relevant data for

9 Corpus Christi College, Oxford. Langdon maps, 1616.

10 These acreages are calculated from the Langdon map that shows field boundaries. These boundaries are essentially identical with the boundaries in the Tithe map of 1842, (Appendix 1, Map 7), because fields were demarcated by hedges and farmers seldom chose to lift and replant hedges, unless it was essential. The Tithe award gives the approximate acreages of each field.

11 Hampshire Record Office 33M71/P1.

12 Hampshire Record Office 67M80/PD1a&b.

Newnham farms as they are currently named is given in the accompanying tables. I have however taken the liberty of including Owens Farm[13] because we have a great deal of background information, as discussed above.

1841 FARM DATA[14] [15]

Farm	Farmer	Acreage
Manor Farm	John Rogers	137
Newnham Green Farm	Richard Tubb	52
Naish's Farm	John Wise	52
Owens Farm	William Kimber	116

Besides William Orford and David Smith having two occupations, it seems possible that the Rev Richard Hunter (Rector of Newnham from 1816 to 1844) may also have been involved in farming the 29 acres of glebe land that went with the Rectory. The point of drawing attention to these individuals is to show that some people seem to have been directly involved in farming as well as having other occupations.

1861[16]

Farm	Farmer	Acreage
Manor Farm	John & Thomas Rogers	280
Newnham Green Farm	John Beeston	174
Naish's Farm	John Wise	52
Owens Farm	William Kimber	120

13 Owens Farm was in Newnham until 1932, when Hook was created as a separate civil parish: Owens Farm is now in Hook.

14 Based on information included in the 1841 census.

15 In addition, two shop-keepers, William Orford and David Smith, stated that they also farmed land, 16 and 20 acres respectively.

16 Although not a farm as such, in 1861 Mary Hope, who is believed to have lived at Tithe Barn, formerly Hope Cottage, called herself a farmer of 30 acres. And 20 years later, George Hope claimed to be farming 25 acres.

1881

Farm	Farmer	Acreage
Manor Farm	John Butter	156
Newnham Green Farm	Charles Knight	100
Naish's Farm	Emmanuel Morris	80
Owens Farm	Charles Arman	108

From this it is evident that the tenants, and I believe they were all tenants, regularly changed and they often took on more land if they could get it; as a consequence, one gets the impression that farm sizes changed, but I think this is a false impression. Unfortunately, the data that I have seen does not reveal where the extra acres which are recorded in the censuses were located. The limitations of the census returns also prevent an understanding of whether people with other occupations sometimes farmed a little. For example, it is unclear if the Rector also derived some livelihood from his own farming activity in 1861 or 1881; he had some acres of glebe scattered about the parish, which might have enabled him to grow crops, although it seems more likely that he would have let the fields for rent.

Perhaps the characteristic that stands out most clearly from these acreages is how small the farms were when compared with most current holdings. But one feature that has not changed greatly is the sizes of the fields. This can be seen when comparing current Ordnance Survey maps with the various older maps of our patch, although there is a change – in most cases – to the sizes of the field gateways. In the past an 8-foot or 10-foot gateway would have been adequate for a horse and cart or a two-horse plough team, but modern tractors and their equipment require at least 12-foot gateways and often substantially more. Fortunately, for the moment, our local landscape is still intimate and does not have the prairie-like aspect to be found in some neighbouring parishes.

A digression about some farming changes: cereals

Perhaps the reader will be interested to consider cereal harvesting over the centuries. The 'tableau' below, showing two people cutting corn in mediaeval times, must have been typical throughout Britain. One uses a sickle, the other gathers the cut corn and holds it to make a sheaf. These sheaves were very probably then laid together to form a stook, or 'shock' which is the local Hampshire word.

[17]

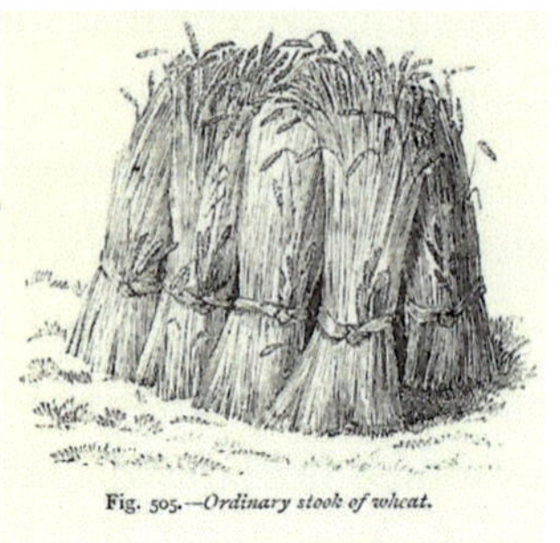
Fig. 505.—*Ordinary stook of wheat.*
[18]

It seems probable that this method of harvesting cereals continued from the earliest times, but even in mediaeval times a team of men using scythes may have replaced people with sickles. The scythe, in skilled hands, could lay the cut corn in swaths that were gathered up into sheaves by men or women, as shown in the picture below.

Fig. 495.—*Mowing corn with the scythe.*

a a a Swathes of corn.
b b b 3 mowers.
c c c 3 gatherers.
d d Open sheaves.
e Bandster binding a sheaf.
f f Bandsters setting a stook.
g Stook.
h Man raker.
i Hand stubble-rake.
k Bound sheaf.

A team of agricultural workers doing all the different harvesting jobs.

17 From a roof boss in Salisbury Cathedral.

18 This and the next two illustrations are taken from Henry Stephens, *The Book of the Farm* (London, 1890 reprinted edn.,) pp. 76, 60 and 83 respectively.

In 1872 the horse-drawn reaper-binder was invented in the USA: one such appliance is illustrated below. At some date thereafter similar machines came to be used in Britain. When they reached Newnham is unknown, but the reaper-binder was the harvesting equipment with which I was very familiar in the 1940s.

As a result of these labour-saving devices being widely used, it was no longer necessary to have teams of people using scythes. However, it was still necessary to have several workers to gather up the sheaves to make the stooks: each stook comprised eight sheaves. During WW2, when there was a shortage of manpower on the land, villagers would enter the fields and do the stooking when they got home after work.

This picture shows a horse-drawn self-binder that cut the crop, gathered it and tied it in bundles of sheaves. These sheaves were then dropped off in groups of eight to facilitate building the stooks.

The photograph overleaf shows Joan King (now Mrs Cutcliffe), granddaughter of William Grinter of Manor Farm, Newnham, driving his tractor in about 1947. It demonstrates how the self-binder had changed little but tractors were replacing horses.

In 1943 I very clearly recall Stan Grinter (the son of William Grinter) cutting a swath all round a field of wheat, using a scythe and binding up each sheaf using some of the straw which he had cut. Then – probably next day – Stan and his father came in to cut the corn using a self-binder. Bill Grinter managed the horses while Stan stood on the platform and released the bundle of sheaves, at intervals.

Photograph courtesy of Mrs Joan Cutcliffe

If problems arose, he signalled to his father, by pulling on a string that was round Bill's right arm. He would then stop the horses so that the problem could be resolved. There wasn't always a problem and several times I saw Stan stop his father; then, using a catapult, he aimed at a rabbit squatting just out of danger from the cutting blade. Stan was a brilliant shot with a catapult and almost invariably leapt down from the platform to pick up a stunned or dead rabbit.

By 1952 the self-binder was becoming obsolete and being replaced by towed combine harvesters. These were much the same small size – say a 6- to 8-foot cutter blade – as the self-binder, but they threshed the corn as they harvested the crop and threw out the straw; they also scattered the chaff – corn husks, weed seeds and other rubbish, with a certain amount of grain depending on their efficiency. The threshed corn flowed through two chutes into West of England sacks (220 lbs – heavy!) As the first sack filled, the switch was turned to fill the second sack and the first sack was quickly tied off at the top. Then at intervals the man on the platform (sometimes me) dropped off several sacks together to make collection easier at the end of the day. Currently, of course, there are monster machines that cut wider and faster, and can store the threshed corn on board to be discharged into trailers that follow round the fields.

The speed at which harvesting techniques have changed in the past century and a half is astonishing. The teams using sickles or scythes were replaced in my grandfather's time (1850–1932); I have seen the horse-drawn self-binder replaced by enormous combine harvesters in the past 70 years.

All these changes in cereal harvesting techniques have compelled farmers to alter their own way of harvesting wheat and barley crops; oats also, but oats do not seem to have been much grown in Newnham in my lifetime. I believe that in the early twentieth century wheat always had a ready market for biscuit- and bread-making, especially during the war (1939–1945) and thereafter. Barley used to be important for beer production and to a lesser extent for livestock feed. Oats were chiefly grown for horse feed and, as machines took over from horses, the demand for oats declined. What of maize or field beans or oilseed rape? Back in the 1940s and 1950s, I think maize was never considered and it has only become a major crop since green silage for cattle came into fashion in the 1960s. Field beans, again often for horses, were always grown hereabouts, but the market has declined. Oilseed rape was almost unheard of until rather late in the twentieth century, and the bright yellow spring/summer fields were never, I think, seen round here before then.

Reverting to changes in harvesting techniques before combines, wheat and barley were usually cut when almost ripe and allowed to finish ripening in the stook. The stooks could stand in the field for some weeks if the weather was unfavourable and usually did not deteriorate. The only real risk was damage from hordes of sparrows, chaffinches and other small birds, as well as rooks, crows, jackdaws and pigeons, which fed daily on the ears as they were so accessible. Rats and mice also took their toll. In the 1700s the losses so alarmed the Newnham churchwardens (who were also farmers) that in most years between 1765 and 1797 they paid two pence per dozen sparrows killed.[19] But there was another sound reason for leaving the stooks, at least for a time: not only could the grain become fully ripe, it could – subject to the weather – dry out. If the crop were to be made into a stack when the moisture content was above 15%, the stacks could smoulder and catch fire – itself a disaster. So once the sheaves were dry enough to be gathered up, they were loaded onto a large cart by two men pitchforking them up to someone on the cart. The latter's job was to lay

19 Hampshire Record Office 67M80 PW1.

them with the ears inward and the butts outward, starting at one end of the cart and working all the way round, piling the sheaves ever higher. It was hard work – I've done it. The sheaves were then unloaded and built into a stack on the edge of the field by a gate, or in the stack yard on the farm. At some later date, a threshing machine contractor would go round from farm to farm and thresh the sheaves, leaving behind a pile of straw and a heap of 'tailings' which were chiefly husks and weed seeds, but also an amount of grain, depending on the efficiency of the equipment. These tailings attracted flocks of birds to feed.

With the coming of combine harvesters, the process has changed dramatically. The crop has to be fully ripe and preferably of less than 15% moisture content. If the moisture content is higher, the corn has to be dried – a further expense for cereal farmers who must now have drying equipment.

The whole harvesting activity has also changed over the years. The picture of men scything the crop, others gathering the sheaves and others stooking indicates a huge requirement for manual labourers. The self-binder reduced the need for farmhands in the fields, but even so, during WW2, and until the combines came in, many in Newnham turned out in the evenings to help stook the sheaves. It was, incidentally, rough work because one's forearms were 'shredded' by the thistles that often infested the crop. Those were the days long before selective weed killers were introduced, so the fields were full of weeds. But another, more entertaining, activity was also a regular feature in the war. The corn was cut by the self-binder going round the field in ever-decreasing circles, so that the many wild rabbits were steadily confined to a reducing square at the centre. Anyone from the village might come hoping that a rabbit would rush out near them which they could knock over with a stick; during the war, we were all short of meat and it was a chance to improve the family's diet. Nowadays, modern machines do not circle the fields; instead they drive up and down. There is no longer a square of uncut corn, and the rabbits escape to the side long before the combine has finished. Today it is only the kites and buzzards which benefit as they swoop down upon the escaping vermin.

Another farming change: winter livestock fodder

Another of the major changes in farming in the last 70 years has been the storage of winter fodder for livestock. Formerly, the bulk of food for livestock in winter was hay, which tended to be cut in June or July, subject to there being a favourable week of dry weather. Because the weather in the summer cannot be depended on, scientists began to look for ways to preserve green grass for livestock feed. About 1945 the technique of silage-making was developed, by excluding air from stored green grass (and chopped maize, later). The technique was taken up in Britain after WW2, and is now the standard method of feeding cattle in winter.

There are photographs which show two aspects of haymaking and storage at Newnham Hill in 1934 (**Figs. 8** and **9**). And to demonstrate how technology has changed in the past 80 years there are two photographs taken at Newnham Hill in 2014 (shown in **Figs. 10** and **11**).

Mixed farming

Since WW2, local farms have tended to specialise in either arable or livestock, and sometimes in 'horsiculture'. But this was not the situation in the past; as explained above, in the 1500s and 1600s and for the next 300 years, farmers were hedging their bets with a mix of livestock and arable crops and they often manufactured end-products (what we might regard as 'added value') for sale from the 'farm gate', e.g. cheese, butter and bacon. These were additional to any surplus of wheat or barley and of course those livestock that were not required for breeding. Now, in and around Newnham, there is very little mixed farming.

Besides the major modifications in cereal and grass harvesting, and the type of farming practised near here over these last 70 years, there have been many other farming changes: new ways of ploughing and sowing crops, the use of herbicides, insecticides and fungicides, the precision application of fertilisers, satellite guidance of farm machinery. But this is not intended to be a treatise on farming – the point I am making is that farming has changed enormously from being highly labour-intensive to requiring more and varied, and usually very big, machines. These in turn need larger fields, almost prairie-like, and the consequent removal of hedges. It has become much more efficient, but it has also altered the landscape and the ecology, often resulting in habitat change and sometimes the loss of wildlife that we have been used to. It is the price we pay for demanding cheap food – we mustn't blame the farmers. It is we who are to blame.

Earlier, attention was drawn to how harvesting, before the coming of the self-binder, greatly relied on manual labour. The self-binder removed the need for workers using scythes and sickles; however, there was still a need for extra casual help to bring in the crop. The picture is perhaps most clearly delineated by comparison of the nineteenth and early twentieth century census returns. The figures below show how the number of agriculturally occupied people has reduced since 1801:

Census year	Population	Number in Farming	Percentage in Farming
1801[20]	135	30	22%
1841	164	34	21%
1861	160	33	21%
1881	165	29	17.5%
1901	229	16	7%

Writing in 2024, it is believed that only three residents would describe themselves as wholly employed in agriculture or horticulture.[21] The 2011 census of Newnham indicated a population of about 150. Using this figure (which by 2024 had probably grown), the current population employed in Agriculture is perhaps 2%.

Commons and Commoners' Rights

Before leaving farming, it is important to draw attention to the fact that formerly there was a driftway[22] from Newnham Green to Hook Common. The latter area, together with Newnham Green and the driftway, are the only sections of

20 1801 Census, Abstract of the Answers and Returns (1802), p. 318. Newnham. These estimates are for the 'core' of the village (i.e the dwellings round Newnham Green, Lyde Mill and the part of the Barracks then in Newnham). The Census Act 1800 was an Act of Parliament which enabled the first census of England, Scotland and Wales to be undertaken. The census was carried out in 1801 and has been repeated almost every ten years thereafter.

21 The 2011 census showed that Newnham, Nately Scures and Water End had a population of 518, of whom 49 residents were in care homes, leaving 469 in private dwellings There were then 229 private dwellings, of which 74 were in the core part of the civil parish or 32 %. This percentage of 469 inhabitants suggests that Newnham's population was about 150.

22 A broad lane or narrow country road along which cattle or sheep used to be driven to market, or for grazing.

land which until recently would have been subject to Commons' law. At some point, probably when the local Turnpike Act[23] came into force, Newnham Road must have been defined down the middle of the driftway. The land on either side became part of the Commons and Wastes of the Manor. The original driftway is shown on the *c.*1700 map[24] (Appendix 1, Map 5) and on the Tithe Map of 1842[25] (Appendix 1, Map 7) From studying these maps, and reviewing how the village has grown, it is evident that houses were being built alongside the road on former common land, presumably with the permission of the Lord of the Manor. The original funnel-shaped highway can still be seen on recent Ordnance Survey maps. Its purpose was to enable villagers to take their livestock to graze on Hook Common and even as recently as the 1940s some people tethered goats there by day; no villager has exploited such rights for many decades. The cattle sometimes seen on the Common today belong to the Hampshire & Isle of Wight Wildlife Trust with the aim of keeping down the grass and preventing the regeneration of birch trees so as to enable the former wildlife, e.g. nightjars and marsh gentians, to prosper.

As regards Newnham Green, it is said to be a Goose Green, and the late Colonel Jack registered a right to keep ducks on The Green. I believe this right is attached to Elm Cottage where he lived. What other rights have been registered and whether there are other registered commoners is unclear.

Other Recent Changes to the Landscape

Although not strictly a farming matter, a major landscape change took place locally about 1975. An aggressive form of Dutch elm disease reached Britain in the 1960s and spread. There used to be elms in the churchyard and on other land in the parish, but they were killed by the disease. They left behind saplings which have grown each year from the trees' root systems, which are not killed; once each of these saplings reaches about four inches in diameter, it is parasitised by elm-bark beetles that spread the fungus and the sapling dies. It

23 'An Act for repairing the Road from Hertford Bridge Hill, to the Town of Basingstoke.' 10 George II, Cap 12. (1737). Hampshire Record Office 44M69/G1/125.

24 Hampshire Record Office 33M71.

25 Hampshire Record Office 67M80/PD1a.

seems that something similar is currently happening to ash trees; ash dieback (*Hymenoscyphus fraxineus*) is another fungus, but one that can be spread by wind dispersal of spores. The landscape is already scattered with dead and dying ash trees and at present there seems to be no resistance to this disease.

CHAPTER 5

INDUSTRIES AND OCCUPATIONS

In the Middle Ages and until the end of the eighteenth century, farming was almost the only occupation of the majority of Newnham's residents. As discussed in Chapter 4 (Agriculture and Local Farming Practice), farm work continued to be the main source of income for 21% of villagers in 1841 and 1861, and still 17.5% in 1881. It was only by 1901 that the percentage of those living in Newnham who were gainfully employed in agriculture fell below 10%. However, from the Middle Ages there were local individuals with other primary occupations; for example, there was a miller at Lyde Mill which 'probably marks the site of one of the two Mills comprised in Mapledurwell in 1086'[1], and perhaps long before. Here the villagers' corn was turned into flour for home-baking, although it is possible that there was a part-time or full-time bakery business within the community. It is also likely that ale could be bought, although home-brewing seems likely to have been commonly practised. We have no record of anyone making harnesses, or of a wheelwright or a wainwright or a blacksmith here at the time; however, some residents may have had these farm-related skills.[2]

It seems certain that some residents had other skills such as carpentry and thatching which would have been required for house construction and repair,

1 William Page (ed.), *A History of the County of Hampshire* (Victoria County History, 1911), Vol. 4, p. 157a.

2 It is possible that these and other trades could be found in nearby villages.

but we have no information about them. We can be reasonably certain that there was a parson living in the village from about 1304, when the first parson, William de Essex, is recorded (Appendix 3, Church Documents (2)), and we know from the 1616 Langdon map[3] (Appendix 1, Map 3) that there was a parsonage house in the village.

Trades

Evidently, by the mid sixteenth century there must have been some local wool-weaving industry into which the presumed wool from local sheep was sold; in 1586, the inventory of William Whitcomb of Newnham reveals that he had wool (15 lbs) and a spinning wheel (see Chapter 4). However, during the seventeenth century there seems to have been a decline in the value of sheep, which suggests that spinning or weaving of wool had ceased to be important here. Clothiers in Basingstoke were complaining in 1631 about competition from Reading, and as a result they were unable to sell their products, and local cloth-makers were ceasing manufacture.[4] Farm inventories at this time show few or no sheep.

Later, the weaving industry around Basingstoke revived: Daniel Defoe visited about 1722, and subsequently wrote that 'Basingstoke is a large populous market town, has a good market for corn, and lately within a very few years is fallen into a manufacture [...] of druggets and shalloons'.[5] The renewal of the weaving trade is reflected in Newnham, where sheep again feature in inventories, and in 1701, Edward Amballin (Amlin), a framework knitter, left 'a working frame for his trade'.[6] Further evidence of weaving comes from several loom weights, which have been found in local fields by metal detectorists: the weights had presumably fallen into the household waste buckets and were spread when manuring the fields.

3 Corpus Christi College, Oxford. Langdon maps, 1616.

4 F. J. Baigent & J. E. Millard, *A History of the Ancient Town and Manor of Basingstoke* (London: Simpkin, Marshall, 1889), p. 411.

5 Daniel Defoe, *A Tour Thro' the Whole Island of Great Britain* (first published in three volumes between 1724 and 1727). Extract taken from Penguin Books paperback edition, 1971, p.187. Druggets are wool or partly wool fabrics formerly used for clothing; shalloons are a lightweight twilled fabric of wool or worsted.

6 Hampshire Record Office AD/01.

From farm inventories, it is clear that besides growing crops and keeping livestock, several farmers had diversified in a variety of ways. Cheese-making, sometimes associated with butter, was being done in the sixteenth and seventeenth centuries by a few farmers; there were others offering flitches of bacon; and two kept bees.

To what extent the coming of the Basingstoke Canal, which opened in 1796[7], affected Newnham is unknown. Possibly some residents benefited by selling goods or services to the navvies who dug the construction, but there is no record. Bearing in mind that the canal is some way away from the village, its impact may have been slight. However, it is clear that Newnham was seriously impacted by the coming of the London & Southampton Railway rail track which reached Hook[8] and Basingstoke in 1838. The digging of the railway cutting rerouted Newnham Road and more or less cut off the Barracks from the rest of the village, a disruption which has left that sub-community largely isolated.

As time passed, new industries and occupations arrived. Our best information comes from the censuses, beginning in 1841. For example, because of the railway, by 1841 there were two railway employees (living in the recently built semi-detached Railway Cottages); by 1881, there were six and by 1901 eight railway employees in the village's other houses.

Then about 1900 the Hook Brick & Tile Company plant was opened on Crown Lane (see Chapter 2), so that in the 1901 census there were seven people employed in brick-making[9] who were accommodated in on-site dwellings. This enterprise closed in 1950.

Other information about employment also comes in the census returns. In 1841, James Lee was a shoemaker living in Manor Farm Cottages. In the 1891 census, William Gubby, perhaps living in Valentine Cottage on Newnham Road, is mentioned as a mole-catcher; he had already been recorded in 1878[10] and was still catching moles in 1898.[11] Besides being paid for the moles he caught, a mole-catcher also received money from furriers for their skins.

7 William White, *History, Gazetteer and Directory of the County of Hampshire*, 2nd edn (London: Simpkin, Marshall & Co, 1878), p. 129.

8 There was no station at Hook until 1883.

9 Incidentally, although there was Musselwhite's brickyard already operating in Crown Lane, within Nately Scures, the employees presumably lived in that parish.

10 White's *Hampshire* (1878), *op. cit.*, p. 397.

11 *Kelly's Directory of Hampshire and the Isle of Wight*, (London: Kelly's Directories Limited, 1898), p. 235.

In 1859, John Morris was a shop-keeper and carrier[12] (see Chapter 10); by 1878, he had added coal dealing[13] and by 1891, he was also an oil man.[14] Also in that census, James Brown was recorded as a gamekeeper and in 1901, Morris Maskell was also a gamekeeper.

Commerce

Ale houses have been touched on, and it is probable that in such places the housewife did the brewing and selling, while her husband was employed in farm work or some similar occupation. There is evidence from the Basingstoke Hundred Court Rolls that those who wished to sell their ale needed to have its quality certified, which was done at the Assize of Bread and Ale[15]. The detail of where or by whom this was done is unclear. The date when any specific ale house became a permanent feature of the village is unknown. However, it seems that the Old House at Home, standing at the beginning of Tylney Lane, may have existed by 1725 when the churchwardens' accounts[16] record that Benjamin Poulter paid 1½d for a church rate; in 1739 George Poulter, his son, was paying the same sum, and by 1760 he was paying 3d. By 1787, Ben Poulter was paying 1s 6d (for his 'house') and the same in 1797. We know the site because the 1774 Tylney Estate map[17] (Appendix 1, Map 6) shows that the Poulter family occupied this site. Interestingly, the first mention of the hostelry's name comes in 1878.[18] The advantage of the Poulters' location was because it was the first dwelling on Newnham Green that a traveller coming from Rotherwick or Hartley Wespall would reach where he could find refreshment.

There are likely to have been other ale houses from an early date. It is difficult to be sure when the Crown Inn (now Crown Lodge) became one: it is

12 William White, *History, Gazetteer and Directory of the County of Hampshire*, 1st edn (London: Simpkin, Marshall & Co, 1859), p. 497.

13 White's *Hampshire* (1878), *op. cit.*, p. 331.

14 1891 Census.

15 Baigent and Millard, *op. cit.*, p. 235.

16 Hampshire Record Office 67M80/PW1.

17 Hampshire Record Office 10M48.

18 White's *Hampshire* (1878), *op. cit.*, p. 337.

mentioned in a church rate[19] for 1797, when Sylvester paid and it seems possible his predecessors were Lamble (1787 and 1782) and John Newell (1763).[20] The Crown Inn was ideally positioned for those who had toiled up the steep hill and needed a glass of beer.

At the south end of the village, there was at one time an ale house called the Traveller's Rest; we know this because the building was lost when the railway cutting was made in 1838. Its position was close to where Newnham Road turns sharply eastward when it reaches the railway fence. The plan showing this building's position is held in the Network Rail archives.

It seems probable that there has been a shop somewhere round The Green for centuries, but the first reference to one is in the 1841 Census, when William Orford and David Smith called themselves shop-keepers as well as farmers (see Chapter 4). In the section on Trades above, John Morris described himself as a shop-keeper from 1859.[21] Others also seem to have been shop-keepers; for example, in 1851 George Hope called himself a grocer – I believe his business was in Tithe Barn. The 1881 census tells that James and Martha Lodge ran a grocers' shop from the right-hand end of Crown Lodge. By the 1891 and 1901 censuses, their grocery business may have contracted to some extent; however, in 1898 Martha Lodge was managing a shop and post office[22] – Newnham's Post Office (see Chapter 10). Subsequently, her daughter Gussie Lodge managed the business. In WW2, she sold bottled cordials which were not ration-book items, e.g. ginger cordial, as well as postage stamps. In addition, one could buy dip pens, bottled ink, writing pads with envelopes, and several other household articles. I remember her well: when I first knew her in about 1937 she seemed to be very ancient, although she was probably only in her 50s! But she never seemed to change over the years, and she was certainly fairly ancient, when she died in 1965, aged 82.

19 Hampshire Record Office 67M80/PW1.

20 *Ibid.*

21 White's *Hampshire* (1859), p. 497.

22 *Kelly's Directory of Hampshire* (1898), *op. cit.*, p. 235.

CHAPTER 6

PAMBER PRIORY AND ST NICHOLAS' CHURCH

Setting[1]

St Nicholas' church is associated in perpetuity with Pamber Priory, and indirectly with Monk Sherborne. The association is as follows. Hugh de Port was a close colleague of William the Conqueror, and at Domesday he 'held fifty five lordships of the King in Hantshire [*sic*]; whereof Basing was one, which became Head of his Barony'[2], and 13 others from Odo, Bishop of Bayeux. Hugh also held Sherborne (St John), including a church, directly from the king, and (Monk) Sherborne held from Odo. No church is mentioned in Domesday as being part of Hugh's holding in Monk Sherborne. 'At Hugh de Port's death[3], his son Henry inherited most of his father's holdings in Hampshire, including West and East Sherborne (i.e. Monk Sherborne and Sherborne St John). Henry soon began the process of founding a Priory of Benedictine monks in West Sherborne as a cell or dependency of the Normandy Abbey of St Vigor, Cerisy-la-Forêt.'[4] [5]

1 The history of Pamber Priory has been studied by Moira Grant and written up in *Proceedings of the Hampshire Field Club & Archaeological Society*, vol. 55 (2000), pp. 46–67. Florence Davidson also studied the Priory. Her research can be found in *Proceedings of the Hampshire Field Club & Archaeological Society*, Vol. 7 (1914). I have used both sources when preparing this chapter.

2 William Dugdale, *The Baronage of England*, Tome I of the original 1675 edition, p. 463 (see Appendix 3, Church Documents (1)).

3 In 1096.

4 Grant, *op. cit.*, p. 47a.

5 The Abbey (**Figs. 12** and **13**) lies about ten miles south-west of Bayeux and close to the de Port family home of Port-en-Bessin in Normandy.

Henry's purpose was to ensure that perpetual masses should be said for the souls of King Henry (the First) and his family, and also for his own soul and the souls of his parents, his family and friends. In his foundation charter, Henry de Port donated the tithes of various churches or villages to the Benedictine Abbey; one of these churches was St Nicholas', Newnham.

Pamber Priory's beginning

The foundation of the Priory cannot be dated with any great precision. However, a church building was consecrated by the Bishop of Winchester, William Giffard, who was bishop between 1107 and 1129, although the exact date of the consecration is unknown. It is also unclear how much, if any, of the Pamber Priory building one sees today (**Fig. 14**) had been completed at the time of the consecration. It is not unreasonable to believe the Bishop was actually consecrating the foundation stone (or something of the sort), and that building the Priory had scarcely begun.[6] This consecration may have taken place in 1127. It has been suggested that the parish church of Monk Sherborne, All Saints, might have been the first Priory Church.[7] This would be appropriate, bearing in mind that the purpose of the Priory was to pray for the souls of the King and the de Port families.

The early charters relating to Monk Sherborne Priory are in the possession of Queen's College, Oxford.[8] The first one is Henry de Port's foundation charter, undated, but assigned a date of 1120–1130. In it, Henry granted to God and the Abbey of St Vigor of Cerisy, 'the whole of Sherborne on the west side [*i.e. Monk Sherborne*], its woods, church and tithes.' Also given were the 'meadow of Longbridge and the mill [*presumably Longbridge Mill at Sherfield on Loddon*]

6 Presumably some of the monks could have been helping to build the Priory. If this is correct, prayers for the souls of the Royal family and the de Port families could have begun immediately in All Saints church.

7 'The foundation <u>date</u> of the Priory appears to predate the oldest extant parts of the Priory Church in the twelfth-century tower. Also, the fabric of All Saints predates that of the Priory Church, as demonstrated by the herring bone pattern of the flint. This is an early Norman feature not found at the Priory Church. It is possible therefore that the first Priory Church was All Saints, Monk Sherborne [...] and the Priory later moved to its present (and more suitable) site in the north of the parish.' Grant, *op. cit.*, p. 48a.

8 Extracts from the charters are quoted in Appendix 3, Church Documents (1).

[...] and the churches of Newnham, Bramley and Upton Grey with tithes, and the tithes of Basing'.[9] At Domesday, there were churches in Bramley and Upton Grey, but no church was recorded for Newnham or Monk Sherborne. The last two may perhaps have had simple places of worship for the local communities in 1086, but perhaps not large solid buildings. But in the period after 1086, it is reasonable to suppose that new substantial churches were built in both villages and that St Nicholas' was a sufficiently significant structure for it to be worth donating, together with its tithes. Evidently St Nicholas' was fully functional by 1125.

The second, third and fourth charters omit any reference to Henry de Port. All three are undated (although the third has been assigned a date of 1150–1170), and all of them omit the church and lands in Newnham, presumably because they belonged to Adam de Port, who had inherited the manor of Mapledurwell[10] from his father, Hubert de Port. (The latter is assumed to have been a close relative of Henry de Port.[11]) Adam de Port confirmed, between 1154 and 1172, the Chapel of Newnham and the tithes of Newnham and Mapledurwell to the Abbey of St Vigor, Cerisy.

The circumstances under which Henry de Port gifted St Nicholas', Newnham, when it was part of a kinsman's patrimony, are obscure. It is equally unclear why Henry's father Hugh de Port received 55 manors in Hampshire and his cousin or brother, Hubert, only received one.

Pamber Priory's subsequent history

From its outset, Pamber was considered an 'alien Priory' because its prior's first duty was to the Abbey of St Vigor, and new priors were sent over at intervals from Normandy. It looks to have been fairly well endowed from the beginning, and as time went by new endowments were added. Up to the middle of the thirteenth century the Priory seems to have been economically viable. But during the next two centuries, because of war with France, alien priories were subject to increasing surveillance and were sometimes being suppressed. Pamber continued

9 Grant, *op. cit.*, p. 47a.

10 Newnham was a part of the manor or estate of Mapledurwell in 1086.

11 Dugdale, *The Baronage of England*, *op. cit.*

as a Priory, but experienced difficulties. About 1452 the monks were expelled and Eton College took possession, but soon after that Queen's College, Oxford, emerged as owners of the Priory. It was as a result of the College's ownership that the Rector of Newnham, for the next almost 500 years, was a graduate, often a fellow, of Queen's. Hence our prolonged association with Pamber Priory. To this day, Queen's College retains the right to appoint clergy to our church, now shared with the Bishop of Winchester.

CHAPTER 7

NEWNHAM CHURCH AND CHURCHYARD

The Building's History

There is no record of whether or not the present church (**Fig. 15**) was preceded by an earlier building. However, assuming the new settlement was established in the eighth century, it seems likely that a Saxon church of some kind was constructed before the Norman Conquest. Without appropriate excavation this can only remain speculation. The first reference to Newnham's church is in a charter of Henry de Port when establishing Pamber Priory in West Sherborne, now Monk Sherborne. As noted in Chapter 6, the Priory was dedicated by Bishop Giffard during 1127; it seems likely that this dedication was of a foundation stone. On this occasion, Henry de Port gave certain tithes of Newnham and Mapledurwell to the Priory. It is believed that this gift indicates that Newnham's present church was already built. The fact that Henry de Port did not own the Manor, of which Newnham was a part, has already been discussed, but perhaps Henry had personally funded part or all of the building of St Nicholas', and felt entitled to take the action that he did.

Presumably part of the agreement was that the Priory's monks would support Newnham's church services. The identities of the earliest clergy are unknown but a record of the incumbents from 1304 is given in Appendix 3, Church Documents (2). While the charter gives no dedication for the church, it seems probable that from the outset it was identified with St Nicholas. Certainly it has been St Nicholas' for generations; for instance, the will of Thomas Fielder, dated 1540, requests burial in 'the church of Seynt Nicholas of Newnham' and that of Robert Preston, Rector of Newnham, who died in 1534, requests burial in the chancel of St Nicholas, Newnham.[1]

The chancel arch is in the Norman style with dog-tooth decoration typical of its period and has been dated to about 1125.[2] Over the subsequent centuries, there is no written information about how the church may have been modified. It is very unlikely that the ground plan has changed at all since the church was built, although certain features may have been modified before the major restoration in 1846–47. For example, any small Norman windows may have been brought 'up to date' and replaced with windows in the Early English style, but that is academic, because the major adjustments in the nineteenth century removed any earlier changes. In fact, the nave's dimensions before the modifications only differ very slightly from those visible today.[3] It seems certain that the nave walls stand where the Norman builders placed them, and the chancel walls are original. The west window may be an innovation, but we have no information on this point. The most significant outward change to the church was the removal of the wooden bell turret, which was replaced by the tower.

It seems from the churchwardens' accounts that in the eighteenth century the church was tiled, not thatched or slated, and there was a porch.[4] The exact position of the porch is unknown, though the painting of 1832 shows it was not a south porch; a north porch seems unlikely because of the positions of graves which predate 1846. The lists of those who had responsibility for maintaining the post and rail fencing panels which delineated the churchyard record that the Rector had one panel and a gate (roughly halfway along the fence), and that the Malt House had one panel and a gate, but this gate seems to have been at

1 Hampshire Record Office, B/3 and B/37, respectively.

2 William Page (ed.), *A History of the County of Hampshire* (Victoria County History, 1911), Vol. 4, p. 157b.

3 The internal dimensions of the nave before renovation were 41ft 8ins long and 20ft 3ins wide, and the height was 14 ft. (Incorporated Church Building Society 03757, Lambeth Palace Library). Following the 1847 restructuring, the nave measurements have been: length 41ft 7ins, width 20ft 8ins, height to the beam running lengthwise above the windows 15ft 4ins. Page (ed.), *History of County of Hampshire* (VCH, 1911), Vol. 4, p. 157b.

4 Hampshire Record Office, 67M80 A PW1. Churchwardens' rate and account book 1724–1797. References include: 1742–43 '700 tiles 10s' and '10 ridge tiles and sand 2s. 2d.'; 1759 'timber for porch £1. 8s 9d.'; 1763–64 '400 tiles and 18 ridge tiles in total 9 s.'; and 1787–88 'tiles and lime for porch 6s'.

the end of the fence, next to the farmyard fence.[5] This suggests that the people attending worship probably walked along the north side of the church (along a track that used to lead into Manor Farm's yard) to a gate that led to a west porch. If this is correct, it might explain why the old shafts and capitals which stand either side of the entrance to the nave have suffered so much weathering: they probably originally stood at the west end of the porch. The old shafts and capitals which stand on either side of the tower entrance were probably part of the inner nave doorway of the original porch. The 1832 painting (**Fig. 16**) shows that there used to be a separate entrance for the parson, which would explain why he was responsible for his own gate leading straight to the door into the chancel. There was at that time no vestry.

The foregoing provides an introduction to St Nicholas' but leaves one major question unanswered: why is the building so much larger than the churches of most other local villages? It is an enigma, so far unsolved.

Description of the Present Church

General

The church is reached from The Green via Church Path. At the entrance to the graveyard there is a tiled oak, flint and stone lychgate, dated 1910.[6] A footpath leads along the south side of the church to the west door. The church comprises a north-west tower, the nave and the chancel; the vestry is below the tower with the entrance from the nave and there is a gallery or organ loft over the west end of the nave, which is reached by the tower's external entrance.

The Bell Tower

The tower dates from 1846–47. Its roof has been described by Pevsner as a sort of Rhenish helm (perhaps influenced by the tower of St Mary's church, Sompting, Sussex).[7] It is surmounted by a weathervane showing a cockerel in

5 A list of those responsible for maintaining the various fencing panels is given in Appendix 3, Church Documents (3).

6 It was given by Mr W. M. C. Pechell and was blessed by the Bishop of Guildford (at that date, a suffragan of Winchester Diocese).

7 Nikolaus Pevsner and David Lloyd, *The Buildings of England: Hampshire and the Isle of Wight* (Penguin Books Ltd, 1967), p. 353.

full crow above the points of the compass.[8] Like the remainder of the church, its walls are of flint with limestone quoins, and there are buttresses at lower levels at all corners.

The architect for the renovation of St Nicholas' in 1846–47 was for long unknown. A Google search of the ICBS (Incorporated Church Building Society) documentation shows that the professional responsible for the extensive restoration of St Nicholas', Newnham, was Benjamin Thorne (who is known to have been working at Basingstoke between 1846 and 1850). He was the surveyor. He was also stated to have been the architect for the refurbishment of St Mary's, Mapledurwell. While it is unclear whether the Newnham surveyor was also the architect, it seems that Thorne very probably performed both roles.

The Bells

The bell ringing platform is reached from the tower's external entrance, up a short flight of stairs. Currently there are six bells. Originally there were three bells, as follows:

- The oldest was a treble (note F[9]), marked with two crosses and *WH*[10] (William Hasylwood, bell founder at Reading, 1494–1509)
- A tenor (note C[11]), marked *Henry Knight made me 1662*[12] (Henry Knight II, bell founder at Reading 1662–1673).
- A tenor (note D), marked *Henry Knight made mee 1602* (Henry Knight I, bell founder 1587–1622).

Latterly these three were chimed, as the tower was deemed unsafe for ringing, and the last occasion they were chimed was Easter Monday 2010 when two bell-ringers (Jeff Ford and Nigel Bell) recorded the sound for posterity; next day the bells were lowered so that the original headstocks and bearings could be renewed, and the bells re-tuned by Whites of Appleton, Abingdon, Oxon. The oldest bell was then 'retired' but has been retained in the church.

8 Given in memory of Colonel and Mrs H. G. Bell.

9 D. A. Holmes, *Towers with three bells or less in the Basingstoke area* (Oxford: J. Hannon & Co., 1979).

10 W. E. Colchester, *Hampshire Church Bells: Their Founders and Inscriptions* (Bath: Kingsmead Press, reprint 1979 of 1st ed. 1920), pp. 9, 10 and 91.

11 D. A. Holmes, *op. cit.*

12 W. E. Colchester, *op cit.,* pp. 36, 37, 38 and 91.

Subsequently three new bells have been purchased and their details are:

- No. 1 (Treble), note G, was formerly at Upper Beeding, Sussex, marked *Mears & Stainbank Foundry, London. Queen Victoria Jubilee 1897, H. D. Meyrick Vicar, G. A. Flowers* [and] *C. Budd. Church Wardens.* It was donated by the Earl and Countess of Buchan. Newnham Church Warden 1993–2010.
- No. 2, note F, was formerly at Shiplake, Oxon, marked *cast by John Warner & Sons Ltd, London 1902.* It was donated by Thomas and Valerie Buckley of Tithe Barn (who left Newnham, 2011).
- No. 3, note E, was also from Shiplake and cast by Warners in 1902.

Additional information about all six bells:

Bell	Weight	Diameter
1	2-3-3	23.50
2	3-0-4	25.00
3	3-1-15	26.50
4	3-3-27	27.25
5	5-0-8	30.13
Retired No. 6	2-1-10	22.75

The weights are given as hundredweight (cwt), quarters (qtr) and pounds (lb). The diameters are given in inches.

The new ring of five bells was blessed on 11 July 2010 and subsequently hung in the tower; a full peal was first rung at a service of dedication on 19 September 2010 in which the Bishop of Winchester participated.

The Doorways

The external tower entrance is twelfth-century work, flanked by undecorated shafts, and it leads up slate stairs to the bell ringing platform, also of slate, and to the gallery. Of interest is the roughly carved cross half-way down the right door jamb; these marks are sometimes thought to be the work of pilgrims.[13] There is also a series of scratches, evidently someone counting in groups of five (sets of four vertical scratches struck through by a diagonal).

13 Patricia Dirsztay/NADFAS, *Inside Churches: A Guide to Church Furnishings* (Capability Publishing, 1993), p. 64.

The west door is flanked by twelfth-century shafts and capitals: 'the north capital is carved, with three early volutes, and the other has a small human head with long ears, from which issue two knotted and twisted tails'[14] (**Fig. 17**). The significance of this effigy is unknown, but it may have been a visual reminder to worshippers that they should leave their fears of the supernatural outside the church and concentrate on spiritual matters, because they were entering God's house.[15] The rest of the doorway is modern. A cursory inspection shows that both shafts to the doorway are well-weathered, which suggests that they were part of the outer doorway of the former porch. The architrave of the original porch was perhaps decorated in the Norman style, but because it faced the prevailing wind and rain the stonework had probably deteriorated. Consequently, during the repairs in 1846–47, the new architrave that we see today was put in place.

The doorway into the vestry is believed to be the original doorway which enabled the parson to enter the chancel from outside the building. We know there was such a doorway because it is visible in the painting by Chevalier Grant (**Fig. 16**). It is of interest that the doorway stones show that they were dressed using an adze.

The Nave and Chancel

The interior of the nave is dominated by the chancel arch (**Fig. 18**), almost 7ft 6ins wide and 10ft 8ins to the top of the arch, set in a massive wall. The arch itself is emphasised by the concentric outer curves and the four-inch-wide band of dog-tooth Norman carving, and by the high roof above. At each side of the arch are detached shafts (or columns) resting on two rolls and with cushion capitals. Long ago, features on both sides of the arch were deliberately destroyed. There is no record of what was there before, nor is there any record of when or why these features were destroyed. The destruction suggests that more than one incident of anti-church feeling may have resulted in the damage at the top of the left shaft which was subsequently painted over with a red ochre-coloured paint (**Fig. 19**); this suggests that the damage was done before

14 Page (ed.), *History of County of Hampshire* (VCH, 1911), Vol. 4, p. 157 b.

15 There is a carving on the left shaft at the entrance to St Swithun's church, Nately Scures, which may be giving the same message to worshippers. It is of a mermaid: mermaids represented water spirits and therefore supernatural beings.

1538[16], because the practice of painting on church walls was discontinued after the Reformation.

A second feature, at the top of this shaft, seems to have been destroyed at what must have been a later date, because there is no paint decoration. Likewise, some piece of stonework seems to have been removed at the top of the southern or right-hand shaft: we have no record of what was demolished. However, fortunately the unusual effigy of a face with long ears (**Fig. 20**) (reminiscent of the capital of the right-hand shaft at the church's entrance) remains in place, undamaged, as it has done for centuries. This effigy may also have had the function of reminding worshippers to leave behind any un-Christian ideas on entering the chancel.

The stonework on both sides of the arch was in the past decorated with what are now very faded scrolls – possibly depicting the Tree of Life? The same coloured paint can also be seen on some of the re-used stones around the nave's south facing windows, which suggests that red ochre was often used in St Nicholas' in earlier times. *En passant*, we can be sure that the walls, or at any rate some of them, were decorated with biblical scenes which would have been used by the parson to illustrate points that he wished to make during his sermon. This was a common practice from mediaeval times when there were no books which the congregation could read. At the Reformation these sorts of pictures were hidden with whitewash but careful cleaning in some churches has revealed the original paintings.[17]

As one sits in the nave, one gets a sense of strength and solidity because of the thickness of the Norman wall dividing the chancel from the nave, but it is clear that the other nave walls are themselves of equal solidity as they too are at least three feet thick. There is no ceiling to the nave, but the substantial wooden beams, which hold the roof, add to this sense of strength and permanence. These beams have not been dated by dendrochronology, but if this scientific technique were to be used to investigate their age, it might be found that some of them are original and were reused in 1846.

16 If this damage was done before the Reformation (say, 1538) it *may* have been caused by dissidents such as the Lollards who were active from about 1375 to about 1430; they protested the veneration of images and material things in the Church. Perhaps the top of the shaft was decorated with the likeness of a saint, which led to the damage we see today. There is some evidence that Lollards were 'active in the northern part of Hampshire' (including the Basingstoke and Odiham areas). See Charles Kightly, *The early Lollards: A Survey of Popular Lollard Activity in England 1382–1428* (University of York, PhD. Thesis, 1975), p. 328.

17 For example, at St James' church, Bramley, Hampshire.

As one mounts the step on entering the chancel, a notch can be seen in the arch on each side, where, formerly, there must have been a rood screen. Within the chancel, the north, east and south walls are almost the equals of the nave. The roof is substantially lower and the walls closer together. Within this setting, the old-style undistinguished pews – the former choir stalls – and the chequer-board black and white marble floor, give a sense of intimacy. This is reinforced on cold winter mornings at early service, when the velvet curtains are drawn together to reduce the draught.

The furnishings of the church are 'modern'. A plate on the pulpit records that the refurbishment of the interior, including the pulpit, prayer desk and pews, and also the east window, were completed by Christmas 1892. The reading lectern was given at Easter 1910. The altar was given in 1920 (in memory of Capt. G. A. Maconchy, 5th Royal Gurkha Rifles, killed in action in Waziristan, 1920). In subsequent years, further gifts and some changes have been made.

The kneelers were made by members of the parish in the early 1980s. The red hessian carpet in the nave was purchased about 2000 and the red woollen carpet around the font and leading to the pulpit was bought (with funds supplied by Basingstoke Borough Council) in 2023.

The Windows

All the north windows, and the single south window of the chancel, and the west windows in the gallery and the tower, are of clear glass, which allows maximum light into the building. The east window (**Fig. 18**) was given by Mrs Helen Wylie in 1892; she was the widow of the Rev George Wylie (1845–1879). It was made by Alfred Octavius Hemming[18] and replaced a painted glass window dated 1731–33, which had shown Christ on the road to Emmaus. The present window represents the Ascension of Christ into Heaven, with two angels holding a scroll bearing the words 'Ye men of Galilee why stand ye gazing up into heaven?'[19] The scene is of a stylised Jerusalem with the 11 disciples in two groups looking upward at Christ; there are nine other angels in white, and a further 11 angel faces depicted in red glass.

18 I am grateful to Mr Rodney Hubbuck, who wrote 'The stained glass of the east window [...] is by A. O. Hemming.' The reference is in *The Building News*, 60 (1891) p. 494. '[*Hemming's*] most prominent work must be in the Chapter House at Canterbury Cathedral.'

19 The Acts of the Apostles 1:11.

In the nave, on the south side, the most easterly window is composed of a frame enclosing individual glass lozenges with four motifs: fleurs de lys, vine leaves, oak leaves and a cruciform flower, perhaps dogwood – a symbol of the Crucifixion. The central window shows Christ with a scroll above and the words 'Come unto me all ye that labour'.[20] It was given in loving memory of William and Anne Maria Goring, late of Sheldon's[21], Hook. The most westerly window depicts Christ holding a small child with four others crowding around; underneath are the words 'Suffer the little children to come unto me.'[22] It was given by the Rev Andrew Wallace Milroy (Rector, 1879–1889) to record the baptisms of his family. By local tradition, the children's faces in the window are likenesses of his five offspring.

Memorials – the Nave

There are several memorials on the nave's walls. The first on the north side is to the Rev George Wylie and his wife Helen; during his 34 years as Rector, he masterminded the renovation of the church in 1846–47. Some feel his Victorian zeal was excessive and that we have almost certainly lost several features of historic interest, for example, earlier memorials[23], and perhaps markers for graves of those buried in the nave or chancel.[24] The next plaque commemorates the Rev Charles Henry Coryndon Baker DD who was rector from 1901 to 1916.

On the west facing wall of the nave, over the prayer-desk is the 1914–1921 Memorial to those who died in or as a result of the Great War, 19 names in all.[25] Then adjacent are the names of the six Royal Engineers, who died while trying

20 St Matthew 10:28.

21 Sheldon's was located approximately where Sheldon's Orchard, off Middle Mead, Hook, is today; the house was razed in May 1985. The Goring family owned and lived at the farm from 1853 until William Goring died aged 47, on 12 February 1879.

22 St Mark 5:14.

23 Most old churches have memorials on the wall, usually to parsons, but sometimes to benefactors, and these can date back at least to the 1600s. These were sometimes of an elliptical design with raised edges. While making repairs to the tower during 1990, the stonemason found a fragment of the decorated elliptical stone moulding which must once have graced the nave. Unfortunately, it was too small to carry a name.

24 For example, the 1534 will of Robert Preston, Rector of Newnham, requests burial in the chancel of St Nicholas, Newnham: Hampshire Record Office 1534 B/37.

25 The names of the fallen are: W. J. Champion, A. J. Clark, H. Englefield, A. V. Fitchett, W. Gubby, A. Holdup, E. J. Holdup, H. C. Lane, W. G. Lane, J. Lever, G. A. Maconchy, T. M. Marker, F. G. Matthews, S. J. Morris, V. Morris, C. H. Stent, F. Stringer, J. Willis, H. Young.

to defuse a bomb on the railway line.[26] They are also commemorated by a plaque next to the railway bridge on Crown Lane (see Chapter 2).

Next, the south wall of the nave: there is a pulpit light given in memory of Fanny Vernon Harrop. Then, beside the pulpit, there is a memorial to the Right Honourable Sir Frederick John Wrottesley, Kt, who lived at Manor Farm from about 1925 until he died in 1948: he may be the only resident of the village to have featured in the Dictionary of National Biography.[27] There follow further memorials, Georgiana Pechell (née Harrop) and two of her infant grandchildren, Aimée and Estelle Pechell, then William Mortimer Charles Pechell and his wife Emily Louisa Pechell.

If armorial bearings are memorials, then St Nicholas' displays those of George I, painted on wood. This coat of arms used to hang from the front of the gallery, but was banished to the tower for many years. Fortunately, the churchwardens in the late 1980s arranged for the paintwork to be refurbished[28] and it hangs once more in the nave. Displaying the Royal Arms was a sign of loyalty to the Crown; a further display of loyalty was ringing the church bells to mark the anniversary of the Coronation and again on 5 November (Guy Fawkes Day). This used to happen regularly in Newnham during the eighteenth century[29], and may have been a tradition in earlier times.

Memorials – The Chancel

On the north wall, a tablet commemorates the death in 1781 (aged 38) of Jane Richmond, wife of the rector; and also of her husband, the Rev Joseph Richmond DD who died in 1816, aged 97: he was the incumbent here for an astonishing 54 years. On the chancel floor, a flagstone records them as JR 1781 JR DD 1816.

On the north wall of the sanctuary is a feature which may be unique in Hampshire. It is part of an early fourteenth-century gravestone 'incised with the head and shoulders of a tonsured and bearded priest, apparelled in alb and

26 They were: 2007432 Driver Fred Gaved, 2003661 Sapper Arthur Hill, 1892327 Sapper Ralph R. E. Moxon, 2003625 Sapper Douglas A. Vince, 2004308 Sapper Fred D. Warner, and 2005088 Sapper Arthur White.

27 L. G. Wickham Legg and E. T. Williams (eds.), *The Dictionary of National Biography 1941–1950* (Oxford University Press, 1959), pp. 980–1.

28 Verbal information from the late Mr Patrick G. Hedley-Dent, who was one of those churchwardens; the other was Mr Denys Oppé. They lived at Newnham Green Farm and Manor Farm, respectively.

29 Hampshire Record Office 67M80 PW1. Churchwardens' rate and account book 1724–1797, for example 1730–31.

chasuble, under trefoiled canopy'.[30] The only part of the inscription remaining is '+Hic jacet' ('Here lies'), but the identity of the dead person is unknown. This gravestone was brought to Newnham from Andwell Priory Farm and used to reside on the west wall of the chancel, facing the altar.[31] Its previous position is a clearly visible mark on the wall.

On the south wall, there is a black stone memorial erected by the Rev Paul Daniel Eyre (Rector 1889–1899) to his father, the Rev Charles James Phipps Eyre MA, for many years Rector of St Marylebone, and also his brother Ernest Eyre, who died in 1882, aged 22, while still at Christ Church, Oxford. Then to the right of the south window there is a memorial to the Rev Richard Hunter AM (*sic*) who died in 1844, and to his wife Mary, who died in 1840.

A coffin stool inscribed 'Louis and Rosemary' is kept in the chancel. It was given in memory of the Simonds, husband and wife, who lived at Tithe Barn on Newnham Green and who died in 1947 and 1940, respectively.

Memorials – In the Churchyard

Outside the church there are two benches given in memory of Miss Kathleen Close who died in 1960, one by the west door and the other by the lychgate. She lived at Rookswood on London Road, Hook, where Rookswood Close is today. There is also a bench given in memory of Peter Suker, in the north-west corner of the church yard: he lived for a while in Railway Cottage.

The Gallery

The only important feature is the organ, which is inscribed, 'Presented to St Nicholas Church Newnham on January 13, 1952, by Mrs F. E. W. Bell, of Newnham Green Farm (see also the Vestry, below).

The Vestry

This lies at the base of the tower and is accessed from the nave. On the wall is a document prepared by the person who renovated the organ in December 1951, which says, *inter alia*

30 Page (ed.), *History of County of Hampshire* (VCH, 1911), *op. cit.*, p. 157b.

31 W. M. C. Pechell, who lived in Newnham from 1890 until 1932, left a manuscript note: 'This gravestone was moved from the west wall of the chancel before 1890: the bricklayer who helped to move it, Newman, was alive in 1920.'

> *It was made almost 100 years ago [...] It has 268 organ pipes, some wood but mostly metal. The largest is 10 feet long and almost 20 inches in girth, while the tiniest is not as long as a new pencil and less than half as thick.*

The Crypt

There is a crypt under the chancel. The entrance is believed to be under the choir stalls on the north side and was formerly covered by a wooden trapdoor. The wood used to deteriorate because of the damp, and in about 1935 it was replaced by a concrete slab.[32] No recent entry has been made and the present status of the crypt is unknown.

Description of the Churchyard

The original churchyard boundaries can still be traced. If one stands beside the remaining mature yew tree on the path from the lychgate to the west door of the church, two ridges are clearly visible going towards Manor Farm's fence, one to the south of the church and one to the north. Chevalier Grant's painting of the church (1832, **Fig. 16**) shows that there was a post and rail fence along the boundary to keep livestock out of the churchyard.[33] This original burial plot has been added to at various times. A piece of glebe, on the south of the boundary and adjoining Crown Lodge, was gifted by the Rev Joseph Richmond about 1800. Then in 1923, there was an extension to the north gifted by Major Sir Herbert Cayzer (later 1st Baron Rotherwick); this was consecrated in 1924.[34] In 2000 a further parcel of land at the north-west corner was given by Mr Colin Lewin of Manor Farm. To the east of the Cayzer extension and by the lychgate, there is a memorial garden given by the late Mrs Jean Oppé, also of Manor Farm, in 1997. These extra sections of land were given because the rest of the churchyard was filling up with graves.

32 Verbal information from the late Mrs M. Mortimer Bell, daughter of Mr W. M. C. Pechell.

33 The Churchwardens' accounts and Overseers' accounts between 1766 and 1835 (Hampshire Record Office 67M80 PW1 and PO1) reveal that the responsibility for maintaining between one and four panels of the fence rested with specific individuals or with specific properties: details can be found in Appendix 3, Church Documents (3).

34 Hampshire Record Office 21M65 DD 263. Diocesan Deeds, Newnham.

A 'back-of-the-envelope' calculation suggests that since 1066, between 1,000 and 2,000 people have probably been buried in the churchyard. This calculation is based on the estimated population numbers in Chapter 3, and then assuming a fairly high death rate, particularly among children, and perhaps wives when giving birth. The calculation also assumes that Newnham had a church here in Anglo-Saxon times. It is not unreasonable to believe that some plots in the churchyard have been used for burials more than once.

This seems an appropriate point to draw attention to the grass path from the steps up from Crown Lane to the west door. There seem to be two significant dips, each about 20 feet long, beginning close to the churchyard's original boundary. A tradition, handed down from my forebears, suggests that these dips may mark the sites of mass graves dug at the time of the Black Death and/or the 1665 Plague. Without investigating by excavation, they must remain a mystery.

Nearer to the church, on the boundary with Manor Farm, is an area which has been set aside for the interment of ashes.

Varied Grave Markers

Our churchyard contains a wide variety of grave markers, or tombstones. The oldest is a very weathered block of granite, and only legible with great difficulty. It records the last resting place of Mary, daughter of Peter Justice, who died 14 August 1728, aged four months. It is likely that her father was the miller at Lyde Mill. The next oldest gravestone is that of Mary, wife of James North. She died on 13 May 1745, aged 37, and she lies under the yews to the south of the footpath. The stone is carved with two pierced hearts on either side of an hourglass, a symbol of the transitoriness of human life.

The fact that the earliest marked graves are dated 1728 and 1745 raises the question as to how the resting places of the dead were previously marked. Gravestones were and are expensive, so graves were marked with a board attached to two stakes (at the head and foot of the grave) and the name(s) of the dead were painted on the board. This kind of marker can be seen in Chevalier Grant's painting. It is only later in the 1700s, carrying on into the 1800s and 1900s that graves came to be marked with tombstones. But of course not everybody chose to use stone. Many chose nothing at all. A tradition developed for nonconformists to use cast iron markers on which were painted the names of the dead – usually black on white (**Fig. 21**). These kinds of markers can be found on the south-east side of the churchyard close to the fence with Crown Lodge. There is another distinctive grave marker between the nonconformist graves just mentioned and the steps from Crown Lane into the churchyard. It may fairly be described as a large chunk of granite, on which is written Edith Burberry[35], who died 8 January 1923 (**Fig. 22**). Moving west, next to the grass path from these steps is a war-grave erected for Private L. R. T. Marriner, RAOC, who died 8 December 1940. He was not a Newnham resident and why he came to be buried here is unclear.

On the other side of the nonconformist graves, towards the lychgate and under yew trees, there is a grave surrounded by a diminutive iron 'fence'. Graves surrounded by metal fences are not uncommon in churchyards, although mostly they are three to six feet high. Further on, towards the lychgate, is the WW1 grave of Sgt S. J. Morris, Royal Fusiliers, who died 10 November 1916. And nearby, slightly obtruding into the pathway itself, is the marker for John Callaway, who died 24 June 1831; his stone bears the verse:

Pray look on me as you pass by,
As you are now so once was I.
As I am now so you must be,
Prepare yourself to follow me.

Then, to the north within the land given by Sir Herbert Cayzer, there are other graves, which are interesting in their own right. There is a grave marked with a cross embellished with an angel, and nearby is a grave marked with a broken pillar, a symbol of the transience of life (**Fig. 23**); nearby there is a very typically Scottish gravestone which begins 'Erected by Alexander & Margaret Macintosh in memory of [...] James Alexander Macintosh [...], killed in action 8 March 1941.'[36]

Near the west end of the church, there are gravestones marking members of three former farming families. Immediately to the south of the church's west door are graves belonging to the Webb family. The 1774 Tylney map (Appendix 1, Map 6) indicates that the Webbs occupied Manor Farm at that time, and it

35 Edith Burberry was very probably the daughter of Thomas Burberry, the inventor of the waterproof coat, who lived at Crossways, Hook (where the surgery car park currently is).

36 Most gravestones begin with the name of the departed, and not with the name of the person erecting the gravestone.

seems probable that John Webb, who died in 1830, was the last of the family to farm there. He was born in 1781, and his wife, Fanny (née Parsons) was born in 1779; she died in 1877 aged 98! She and her sister Mary Parsons share the same grave; Mary was 95! The Webb graves often have long stone stretchers over them to prevent the body-snatchers or resurrectionists.[37] Then to the north of the tower are markers for the Rogers' and Rowlands' families. The Rogers were at Manor Farm during the 1840s to the 1860s (see Chapter 4). The Rowlands may have been farming Naish's Farm between 1796 and 1816 and possibly later, but the evidence is inconclusive. Both the Rogers' and the Rowlands' graves were obviously very quickly bricked over, presumably to prevent body-snatchers. To the north-west of these graves are those of John Cooper (died 1795) and John Marsh (died 1801), both of which tell that they were farriers. It is sad how seldom people have their livelihoods recorded on their memorials.

In Newnham churchyard, one can find many different sorts of grave markers, some indicating the transience of life, some indicating life's clear termination, some are in enclosed plots, most are of stone (granite, limestone, sandstone – pale, natural colours, and sometimes black), some are cast-iron, one or two are of roughly hewn rock. About the only style that is missing is a tabletop. We have a very interesting churchyard.

One general point which may be worth making is that sandstone is a very poor material for marking graves. This is because over the course of time rain penetrates the stone, and when there are frosts parts of the stone tend to crumble away; this is particularly true of the carved area so that names and dates are permanently lost.

Church Path

The foregoing detail about the description and occasional history of our church and churchyard would be incomplete without some reference to the Church Path. The short length of roadway from The Green to the lychgate is sign-posted Church Path. This has been mentioned in Chapter 2, by its official name Footpath No. 3. This is a very prosaic name for a public right-of-way which year by year has known the regular footfall of hundreds of people: mainly they would have been worshippers from Hook going to and from St Nicholas' church for

37 Resurrectionists were body-snatchers who stole corpses from graves and sold them to the medical profession for dissection.

Sunday, and other services. In more recent years, most have walked this path for exercise and social reasons.

Since at least Domesday, and until the 1800s, Newnham was an ecclesiastical parish of two parts. Originally the main settlement was clustered round The Green, with a secondary part in what is now Hook; the latter was a scatter of farms plus Whitewater Mill: farms such as Owens Farm, Sheldon's (a.k.a. Sherlands), Lee's Farm, Hook Farm, Searle's Farm and Titchenor's Farm, together with a grouping of dwellings and small businesses where the London–Basingstoke and Reading–Odiham roads cross.

In mediaeval times, the Church expected everyone to attend church every Sunday and also on the several saints' days each month. This was not such a burden as it may seem, because the people were keen to take part in order to maintain a good relationship with God. This was at a time when there were no medical facilities such as we understand them, and the Grim Reaper might strike with little or no warning. During the Middle Ages, as well as through Tudor and Stuart times and up to the nineteenth century, there were no explanations about the origins of sicknesses. Diseases like influenza, plague, smallpox, leprosy, cholera, diphtheria or tetanus, were not understood and were often explained as signs of God's anger. People went to church to keep in touch with God.

With this in mind, it is rather easy to understand why those living in Hook wanted to attend St Nicholas' which was their only church until 1886 when a mission church was built[38], where Elms Road meets the A30 in Hook. It was mainly of corrugated iron and was vulgarly called the Tin Tabernacle. In mediaeval times and subsequent centuries, most people had to rely on getting to church on foot. The road from Hook was essentially unmade up, and often the surface was broken up by cattle and other livestock, or carts, or people riding on horseback. It must have been very rough, and wet in winter, so from very early on an all-season footpath was created: this started near the Hook War Memorial on Jubilee Green and joined the short roadway in Hook still called *Church Path*. From this point the footpath followed the field hedges (or hedges flanked the footpath) over the fields to Newnham Green. It is now a well-used footpath and was only superseded as a regular means of reaching St Nicholas' church with the coming of bicycles and motorcars once Newnham Road had been improved.

38 *Kelly's Directory of Hampshire and the Isle of Wight* (London: Kelly's Directories Limited, 1927), p. 254.

A detailed study of Church Path has been undertaken by the Friends of Church Path, available at **https://bit.ly/4jmaruL.**

Ordnance Survey Benchmark

Although of no religious significance, it is worth putting on record that near the base of the north-east buttress of the Chancel, facing north, there is a bench-mark.[39] It is in a rather poor state of preservation and not easy to see, probably due to frost damage.

39 Benchmarks are horizontal marks, designed to support a stable 'bench' for a levelling stave to rest on and usually cut into the side of buildings or milestones, which were used by Ordnance Survey between 1831 and the late twentieth century to calculate a height above the mean sea level.

ILLUSTRATIONS

Aerial photograph of Newnham,
reproduced by kind permission of Mick Murnaghan

Fig. 1

Valley bottom before drainage

Fig. 2

Guard at Crown Lane Bridge, 1916

Fig. 3

Pill-box on Newnham Road

Fig. 4

Hollow way on Crown Lane

Fig. 5

Hollow way on Newnham Lane

Fig. 6

David Mitchell MP opening the new bridge built by Old Basing Scouts in 1976. On the bridge were Nigel Bell, John Maltby, Frances Bell and Sophie Maltby and on the bank John Sambrook-Smith and his children. Photograph courtesy of Basingstoke Gazette

Fig. 7

Beehive Farm in 2024: two chimney stacks, scaffolding and rubble

Fig. 8

Hay making at Newnham in 1934

Fig. 9

Stacking hay in 1934.
William Grinter extreme left, Mrs Pechell seated, Montagu Hepper extreme right

Fig. 10

Cutting grass 2014

Fig. 11

Next day, gathering the swaths and blowing the grass into trailers to carry it to the silage clamp

Fig. 12

St Vigor Abbey, Cerisy, Normandy

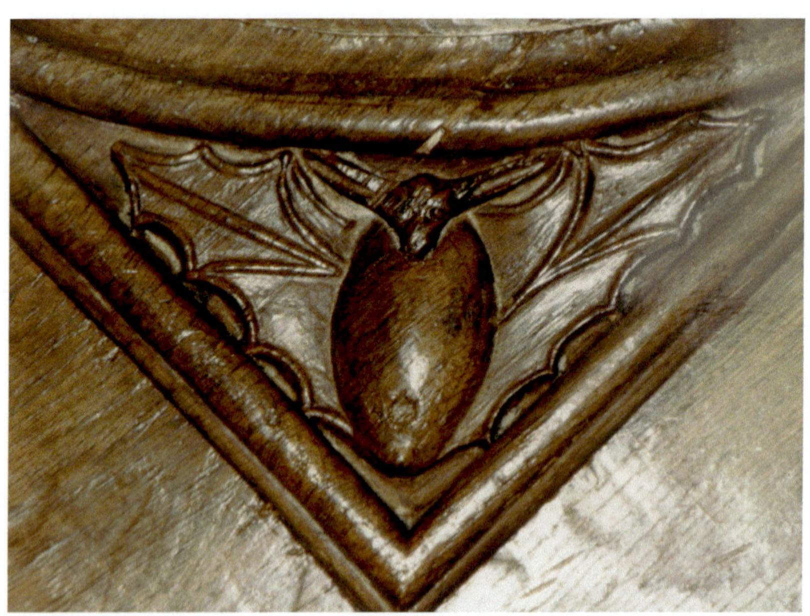

Fig. 13

A misericord from St Vigor's choir stalls, perhaps the inspiration for the carving of the long-eared creature in St Nicholas' church

Fig. 14
Pamber Priory today

Fig. 15

St Nicholas' church today

Fig. 16

St Nicholas' church, by Chevalier Grant, dated 1832. Bishop Charles Sumner commissioned paintings of all churches in Winchester Diocese; these are held in the Diocesan Library

Fig. 18

St Nicholas' chancel arch and east window.
The dog-toothed decoration around the Norman arch is evident

Fig. 19

Left side of the chancel arch, showing damage to the capital; also showing the mediaeval scroll wall painting, possibly depicting the Tree of Life

Fig. 17

The column capital at the west door of St Nicholas' depicting a long-eared creature

Fig. 20

An unusual eared creature topping the column on the south side of the chancel arch

Fig. 21

Cast iron grave markers sometimes used by non-conformists

Fig. 22

The granite block placed in memory of Edith Burberry

Fig. 23

A 'broken column' gravestone

Fig. 24

Manor Farm about 1910

Fig. 25

Hope Cottage about 1910,
showing the central part of the later renamed Tithe Barn

Fig. 26

Tithe Barn today, with right and left extensions

Fig. 27

Naish's farm about 1970,
showing original farmhouse, stabling, cart shed and original barn

Fig. 28

Crown Lodge about 1900 with various extensions; at the extreme right was Newnham's post office

Fig. 29

The Old House at Home, c.1900

Fig. 30

Thorn Cottage, Newnham Road,
before reconstruction as Valentine Cottage

Fig. 31

Newnham Green showing the original red phone-box before its removal by BT

CHAPTER 8

SOME HOUSES

As a rough and ready general rule, houses dating from the fifteenth to seventeenth centuries tended to be built around a central chimney stack, and houses built in the eighteenth and nineteenth centuries tended to be 'hung' between chimney stacks at either end of the house. This seems to work for Newnham.

For this review of the older houses in Newnham it has only been possible to use early maps. Unfortunately, there are only a very few which are useful:

1. Thomas Langdon's 1616 map of the Corpus Christi College, Oxford, land-holding at that time in Newnham, now the fields round Owens Farm. Available as a film strip from the Bodleian Library, Oxford. Illustrated in Appendix 1 (Map 3).
2. The *c.*1700 map of Newnham properties, probably prepared for the church-wardens when assessing the rates payable by landowners or tenants. It is very badly fragmented and incomplete.[1] Illustrated in Appendix 1 (Map 5).
3. The 1774 Tylney estate map, which covers Newnham Green, but it is primarily concerned to show the full extent of the land belonging to Tylney Hall at that time.[2] Illustrated in Appendix 1 (Map 6).

1 Hampshire Record Office 33M71.

2 Hampshire Record Office 10M48.

4. Newnham's Tithe Map and schedule dated 1840–1842.[3] Illustrated in Appendix 1 (Map 7).
5. Ordnance Survey 1877 6 inch:1 mile map. Illustrated in Appendix 1 (Map 8).
6. Ordnance Survey 1881 1:2500 map. Illustrated in Appendix 1 (Map 9).

More detail would probably be available by consulting the deeds of each property. That has not been attempted for this study.

The building in Newnham which, although modified in 1846–47, has stood longer than any other is **St Nicholas'**. Our church has already been reviewed in some detail in Chapter 7. Almost every building in the core of the village is essentially round The Green, and a great many that are of more recent construction have been modified to meet the needs of their owners. In consequence, we no longer retain any building which would give us even a hint of what our earliest houses were like. It is almost certain that these early dwellings were thatched and of wattle and daub construction: a composite building method used for making walls and buildings, in which a woven lattice of wooden strips, *wattle*, are *daubed* with a sticky material usually made of some combination of wet soil, clay, sand, animal dung and straw.[4] However, these structures leave a very small footprint and no excavation has been undertaken to discover where the earliest houses stood.

Manor Farm Cottage is the next house incorporating early features. A former Director of Planning at Basingstoke suggested that part of it might date from the fifteenth century. The original section is the left-hand side as seen from The Green which looks to have been built round a central chimney stack. Clearly the side that faces Church Path was half-timbered, and it seems likely that between the old structural timbers there was once some wattle and daub, which has been replaced by bricks of varying derivation and age. So far as I know, the house has not been studied by any expert and the beams have not been dated using dendrochronology. The right-hand end of the cottage has been refashioned at a later date, perhaps in the eighteenth century.

Manor Farm was examined, and reported on, in September 1997 by Mr Edward Roberts, the doyen of studies of Hampshire's ancient buildings.[5] He

3 Hampshire Record Office 67M80.

4 Wikipedia

5 Edward Roberts, *Hampshire Houses 1250–1700: Their Dating and Development* (Hampshire County Council, 2003). Manor Farm is not reviewed in this book.

opined that the part of the house facing the church dated from 1500–1550 and the other (west) side was probably built before 1650. The accompanying photograph, dated about 1910 and taken from the church (**Fig. 24**), shows the central part of the house, which was then a farmer's residence. The rest of the building, the newer part facing the church and also the other (west) side was mostly added by Sir Frederick Wrottesley after 1925.

Newnham House, formerly the old Rectory, is shown on the Langdon map dated 1616. Langdon drew perspectives of the houses which he featured on his maps with accuracy and one can see that the 'Parsonage' was already a fairly extensive building. When the Rev Andrew Whelpdale was Rector (between 1658 and 1679), it was assessed for six hearths in the Hearth Tax of 1665. Sometimes the clergy ran schools from their homes, and it is possible that, before Mr Whelpdale's time, a predecessor expanded the Rectory to accommodate residential pupils. In 1725, the (often absentee) Rector, Michael Hutchinson DD, in answer to a question about lecturers in the parish, stated, 'I have a curate who resides constantly in the parsonage, whose name is Thomas Skelton.' He went on to state that 'There is no endowed school in the parish.'[6] This suggests that the Rectory may have been used by the curate, to supplement his income by teaching. By 1788, when there was another Bishops' Visitation, the Rector, Joseph Richmond DD, stated that there was no lecturer and no school.[7]

Tithe Barn (previously called Hope Cottage after the owners in the nineteenth century) was originally solely the central section, a half-hipped cottage with two upstairs and two downstairs rooms plus a kitchen or buttery with cooking facilities at the back (**Fig. 25**). It is believed to have been occupied by Richard Amline in 1586[8], by William Amblin in 1665[9] and by Edward Amlin[10]

6 W. R. Ward (ed.), *Parson and Parish in Eighteenth-Century Hampshire: Replies to Bishops' Visitations* (Hampshire County Council, 1995), p. 96.

7 *Ibid*, p. 304.

8 Richard Amline paid a subsidy of £3/3. See C. R. Davey (ed.), *The Hampshire Lay Subsidy Rolls, 1586*, Hampshire Record Series, 4 (Hampshire County Council, 1981), p. 42. His inventory describes him as a Yeoman in 1621. Hampshire Record Office BO/1.

9 William Amlin paid Hearth Tax for three hearths. See E. Hughes and P. White (eds.), *The Hampshire Hearth Tax Assessment, 1665*, Hampshire Record Series, 11 (Hampshire County Council, 1991), p. 240.

10 The spelling of this family's name is inconsistent and depended on how the person recording the name heard it. Consequently, in different years we find Amline/Amblin/Amlin/Amballin.

who died in 1701[11] (see Chapter 5). The right-hand side of the house, as seen from The Green, was added by Mr W. M. C. Pechell about 1914, and the left-hand wing by Mr L. A. Simonds, after he bought the property in 1935 (**Fig. 26**). Its interior has subsequently been modified.

Naish's Farm is not shown on the 1616 Langdon map, and the land adjacent to Corpus Christi College's holding (now Owens Farm) is marked as Richard Amlin's. That family lived in Newnham for about three generations and, as already mentioned, occupied Tithe Barn. It seems likely that the Amlins were succeeded on this land by Robert Naish, who was assessed for three hearths in the 1665.[12] The *c.*1700 map shows two buildings on this site, perhaps the start of what we see today and the implication is that Naish had already built the original farmhouse, which would explain why he had to pay Hearth Tax. The farmhouse is evidently 'hung' between chimneys at either end. The farmyard was laid out in a style introduced in the late seventeenth or early eighteenth century, with stables and cart sheds to the left of the farmhouse; the barn was opposite the house and cattle sheds were to the right of the house. Two Robert Naishes (Senior and Junior) were each assessed for substantial church rates in 1725. The 1774 map seems to confirm this layout. A new wing may have been added to the southern end during the 1800s, and further changes were made about 1995 (**Fig. 27**).

Newnham Green Farm: the *c.*1700 Newnham map shows what seem to be farm buildings on this site; however, they do not feature on the Tylney Estate map of 1774. The building style of the house, and the layout of its farmyard (much akin to the Naish's Farm layout), strongly suggests that what can be seen today is a replacement of an earlier structure. Without a detailed architectural study, it is only possible to propose a date around 1780–90 for the current building's construction. During the twentieth and early twenty-first centuries the property has been modified, mostly internally.

Elm Cottage: the 1616 Langdon map suggests there was at that time a building on this site, but the *c.*1700 map does not show any structure; by 1774, there was a dwelling here, which is presumably the cottage one sees today, which was formerly two cottages.

11 Edward Amballin's inventory in 1701 says he was a framework knitter. Hampshire Record Office AD/01.

12 *The Hampshire Hearth Tax Assessment, 1665, op. cit.*, p. 240.

Crown Lodge (**Fig. 28**) with its centrally placed chimney was probably built in the seventeenth century, and possibly earlier. The history of the building is obscure: what would seem to be this building is visible on the 1774 map; it is arguable from the *c.*1700 map that there was a building on this site. The churchwardens' accounts in 1732/1733 state: 'due from Thomas South to the Parish for the rent of the Church House, £10. 5 s. 0d'.[13] If, and at present it is only speculation, the citation refers to this building, it may have been built after parishioners were banned from trading in St Nicholas' nave. Apparently it was often common practice after morning service on Sundays for trading to take place in churches[14]; however, an increasingly pious approach to the use of churches finally banned commercial activity.[15] Parishes then built church houses for business negotiations and festivities like church ales, and once the church houses had been built, they became the property and concern of the churchwardens.[16] As time passed, the need for church houses declined and these buildings sometimes became private dwellings, inns, schools or almshouses.[17] I believe it is possible that Newnham's church house evolved to become the Crown Inn. The evidence that this could have been Newnham's church house comes from the Duke of Bolton's lease, which records 'All that new erected cottage and little garden [...] being on Newnham Green and adjoining the Church House there' which, in 1722, was rented to 'Richard South, victualler'.[18] Photographs taken in 1900 show extensions to the right-hand side of the original construction. This added part evidently became Newnham's Post Office (see Chapter 9). After the Great West Road was diverted over Scures Hill (see Chapter 2), the Crown Inn lost trade and was moved (as the Rose and Crown) to Hook Common (now re-named the Hogget). The site (Crown Lodge) was then placed under the care of the churchwardens and was turned into accommodation for five poor families. This suggests to me that originally it was Newnham's church house because the responsibility for church houses often reverted to the churchwardens when they

13 Hampshire Record Office 67M80 PW1.

14 Patrick Cowley, *The Church Houses: Their Religious and Social Significance* (London: Alcuin Club/SPCK, 1970), pp. 20–21.

15 *Ibid*, pp. 22–23.

16 *Ibid*, p. 40.

17 *Ibid*, p. 68.

18 Hampshire Record Office 11M49, lease 13. 441. The Souths renewed their leases in 1737, 1743 and 1767.

ceased to be inns, schools or almshouses. But a *caveat*: the late Stan Waight, who was very good at researching local history and with whom I discussed the matter extensively, was not convinced: there the matter rests.

The Old House at Home originally (**Fig. 29**) had a thatched part at the back of the brick-built front which we see today. There seems to be a building shown on the 1700 map. There is clearly a structure on this site on the 1774 map, when George Poulter is shown as occupying the land. The thatched part caught fire around 1904, and must have been destroyed, although the brick front was obviously saved. It seems likely from the churchwardens' accounts that the Poulter family were already occupying this land in 1725. At that date, Ben Poulter was assessed for a church rate of 1½ d.

Woodside was originally two dwellings, probably for workers on Newnham Green Farm. It does not appear on any early Newnham map, e.g. the Tylney 1774 map, but it does feature on the 1842 Tithe Map.

Bridleway: like Woodside, this consisted of two dwellings, perhaps for Newnham Green Farm workers. It is not on the Tithe Map, but is on the Ordnance Survey 1877 6 inch:1 mile map.

Lyde Mill: the Mill 'probably marks the site of one of two mills comprised in Mapledurwell in 1086'.[19] It was described in 1978 as a 'three-storey mill with four bays and a new pantile roof; it has been converted to a private house. The two breast-shot waterwheels are still in position outside the building, but no other machinery remains.'[20] There is some evidence that in 1864 the mill tackle was for sale and perhaps it was no longer a going concern; however, the 1891 census says that James Willis was a miller at Lyde mill, implying that the mill was working at that date. The 1901 census indicated that there was no miller on this site. By 1932, the Ordnance Survey 8 inch:1 mile map indicated that Lyde Mill had stopped working and was disused. In the 1960s the mill itself was extensively remodelled as a dwelling.

Dovecot (a.k.a. **Dove Cottage**) seems already to have been built before 1774, because there seems to be a structure facing Church Path shown on the Tylney Estate Map.

19 William Page (ed.), *A History of the County of Hampshire* (Victoria County History, 1911), Vol. 4, p. 157a.

20 Monica Ellis (ed.), *Water and Wind Mills in Hampshire and the Isle of Wight* (Southampton University Industrial Archaeology Group, 1978), p. 37.

Valentine Cottage (formerly **Thorn Cottage**), Newnham Road (**Fig. 30**): the 1700 map is probably too fragmented to show whether there was already a building on this site. The 1774 map provides no useful information, bearing in mind that the map was drawn to show the Tylney estate at that stage. The first map to show a building is the Tithe map of 1842. Formerly it was two cottages; it has been extensively modified during the last 70 years.

The **Primitive Methodist Chapel** dates from 1846.[21] At one time there were several nonconformist families in the village. Sadly, the Chapel has not been used for services for many decades. Mr Stan Beavis, who used to live in Newnham View, told me that as a boy, it used to be his duty during the winter to go early to the Chapel on Sunday mornings and light the tortoise stove, so that everything would be warm for the first service at 8 a.m. There would be a second service at 11 o'clock, and a third in the afternoon.

21 *Kelly's Directory of Hampshire* (London: Kelly's Directories Limited, 1927), p. 302.

CHAPTER 9

EDUCATION AND SCHOOLS

What education was available to children (or even to adults) in Newnham between, say, 1086 and 1724 is unknown, but there is a hint in the previous chapter that some pupils were being taught in the Rectory (now Newnham House). If this is correct, it may have begun before 1665. It is clear from the churchwardens' accounts, which begin in 1724[1], that the parish had a literate clerk and that after 1750, when the parish registers begin, the parish clerk was recording, perhaps phonetically[2], births, marriages and deaths of residents. It is possible that individual families could pay for their children to receive some level of learning, perhaps from the Rector or his curate. In this connection, the Rev Michael Hutchinson, Rector between 1718 and 1740, who was often an absentee parson and employed a curate to take services here, wrote in 1725[3]: 'Schools. There is no endowed school in the parish.' This response, with reference to 'endowed' schools, may suggest some kind of teaching was available either in Newnham or nearby. It is worth mentioning that in this same survey, it was recorded that there were

1 Hampshire Record Office 67M80/PW1.

2 For example, the surname Bath can be recorded as 'Baffe', which is presumably how the parish clerk heard it said.

3 W. R. Ward (ed.), *Parson and Parish in Eighteenth-Century Hampshire: Replies to Bishops' Visitations*, Hampshire Record Series, 13 (Hampshire County Council, 1995), p. 96, referring to the Episcopal Visitation of 1725.

then three endowed schools teaching 38 scholars and a non-endowed school for 20 girls in Basingstoke, and in Odiham, there was a school for writing, reading and arithmetic taught by Rev William Allen, curate of Dogmersfield. In Rotherwick, Frederick Tylney[4] endowed a school for ten boys and ten girls to be taught writing, reading and arithmetic. Regarding the local position in 1724 and subsequently, although there was no recorded school in Newnham, it is possible that residents could have found ways of having their children educated nearby.

There was a further Episcopal Visitation in 1788[5] which asked: 'What schools are there in your parish? What is the number of scholars?' The Newnham Rector's response was 'None'. Basingstoke had about 38 scholars; Old Basing had one school with '6 poor boys'; Odiham offered education for 20 boys and a further 20 boys for apprenticeships at Robert May's School[6]; and Rotherwick had a school for 20 scholars.

Evidently education up to a certain stage was available in the vicinity, but to what extent Newnham children could take advantage of it is unclear. It is worth pointing out that normally there was a Vestry Meeting in April each year when the churchwardens' accounts were approved. Usually the vestrymen signed the accounts, rather than making a mark, to signify their approval, which may indicate they were at least partially literate; the implication is that most of the larger farmers and some businessmen had received some education.

I am indebted to Edwina Hancock, formerly a resident of Hook, for most of the background information to local education. She prepared an account called 'A Concise History of Hook's Schools' for the Hook Local History Society exhibition to mark the Millennium year 2000. As explained below and in Chapter 2 (footnote 12), until 1932 Hook used to be part of Newnham; and for educational purposes, Hook, Newnham and Nately Scures have developed

4 Frederick Tylney (1652–1725), of Tylney Hall, Rotherwick, was the lord of the manor and a major landlord in the village, his family having owned the manor of Rotherwick since 1629. He served as (a rather inactive) Member of Parliament for various Hampshire constituencies, including Winchester, and built a large mansion, Tylney Hall, as his country seat, but the Tylney family died out in the male line on his death in 1725. The Tylney estate map (Appendix 1, Map 6), though dating from nearly 50 years after Frederick Tylney's death, is important for Newnham background information because it is one of the earliest maps that throws any light on Newnham's evolution.

5 Ward (ed.), *Parson and Parish in Eighteenth-Century Hampshire*, p. 304, referring to the Episcopal Visitation of 1788.

6 A school in Odiham originally founded in 1694 from donations made by Robert May, a local mercer, and still in existence today as a coeducational secondary school with academy status.

together. In 1932, a new separate parish of Hook was created.[7]

As background to the first phases of local education, prior to the early nineteenth century most schools were run by church authorities and stressed religious education. The state became involved for the first time in education in England and Wales from 1833, when Parliament initiated annual grants for the construction and maintenance of schools for poor children; in 1839, a government committee[8] was set up by the Privy Council to administer these grants, which were switched to voluntary bodies and became conditional on a satisfactory inspection. In 1870, the Elementary Education Act was passed, the first in a succession of measures taken between then and the end of the century to make education compulsory for all children between the ages of five and ten. Elected local school boards were created to run schools, which were initially fee-paying, although poorer parents could be exempted. The Elementary Education Act of 1891 made primary education effectively free, and another act in 1899 raised the school leaving age to 12 years.

Formal organised education here seems to have started around 1833[9] when eight boys and eight girls were paid for by the parish at an established school, the location of which is unknown. The 'Elementary School (mixed and infants) [*was*] built in 1843' in (Old) School Road, Newnham, for children in Newnham, Hook and Nately Scures; it was enlarged in 1875 and again in 1895, by which time there were places for 160 pupils and 90 infants.[10] For the record, the 1851 census tells us that Robert Kingham was the National Schoolmaster and his wife Maria a schoolmistress. By 1859, Albert and Martha Jackman are recorded at the National School[11]; in 1878 Mr Joseph Foster is given as the schoolmaster[12];

7 County of Southampton Review Order, 1932.

8 Dr James Kay (1804–1877), a politician and educationalist, was the first secretary of this committee which administered government grants for public education in Britain. Dr Kay – who became Sir James Kay-Shuttleworth in 1842 on his marriage to Janet Shuttleworth, assuming by royal licence his bride's name and arms – devoted the rest of his life to the progress of public education. He was a key figure in the foundation of the Girls' Public Day School Company, and had earlier co-founded a further education college for the training of teachers of pauper children which would eventually become Plymouth Marjon University.

9 Parliamentary Papers 1835 (62) ii, Education Enquiry abstract of the Answers to Returns.

10 *Kelly's Directory of Hampshire and the Isle of Wight* (London: Kelly's Directories Limited, 1927 edition), p. 302.

11 William White, *History, Gazetteer and Directory of the County of Hampshire and the Isle of Wight*, 1st edn (Sheffield: Robt. Leader, 1859), p. 497.

12 William White, *History, Gazetteer and Directory of the County of Hampshire and the Isle of Wight*, 2nd edn (London: Simpkin, Marshall & Co, 1878), p. 337.

and Mr Henry Grimes was appointed the headmaster in 1881[13] (he retired in 1912). Mr George Lawrence took over until he died in 1937. He was succeeded by Mr Harry Budd, who retired in 1949. Mr Bernard Pegler then took over, and in April 1954, Mr Herbert Reece was appointed headmaster. By 1958, school numbers had grown to over 200 children accommodated in seven classrooms, and more temporary classrooms had to be added. By 1965 the school roll had reached 241, and consequently a new school was designed and built on a new site in the middle of Hook. The new school opened during 1974.

Mr Reece retired after 27 years, and in 1982 Mr John Morris took his place, by which time there were 358 pupils on the roll; numbers continued to grow, so that there were 450 children on the roll. The overwhelming majority were from Hook, which had been growing steadily since 1883 when the railway station was opened, with much further housing development since 1971 when Junction 5 of the M3 was opened. At the present time, children from Newnham go to Whitewater Church of England Primary School in Rotherwick, and others go to Hook Junior and Hook Infant Schools. There are also two or three local play schools for the very young. In addition, there are other Newnham children being privately educated at boarding schools.

13 See 1881 census.

CHAPTER 10

SERVICES

Water

The most fundamental service on which any community relies is water. Under the chapter Newnham's Origins, the fact that the community was built on the top of a hill was discussed, and the reliance of all dwellings on wells was referred to. The early Ordnance Survey 1:250 maps show the locations of all natural water sources, rivers and ponds but interestingly, every *well* is featured; this is unsurprising, bearing in mind that the Ordnance Survey was set up by the army to facilitate the movement of troops, and military equipment – hauled by horses or mules – rapidly, all over Britain. A mains water supply is understood to have reached Newnham and Hook school, in Old School Road, in 1910; until that date, all water had been drawn from a well. In Newnham the water situation continued to depend on wells until 1915 when Mr W. M. C. Pechell, who lived at Newnham Hill and also owned Tithe Barn, signed an agreement with the water company (name unrecorded) to extend their water main to Newnham from the school. Thereafter other houses tapped into the supply and most new dwellings were supplied from the main. However, not all existing cottages were immediately connected; those which were unconnected remained reliant on their wells. In fact, when a cottage was let the tenancy agreement usually included wording such as 'The landlord lets and the tenant takes the cottage and garden known as Green View together with the right to draw water from the well which is common to the premises hereby let', or 'The landlord lets the cottage and garden known as the Homestead, together with a right to draw water from the well which is common to the premises hereby let'. These tenancy agreements date from 1939 and 1941.

Sewage

So far as I am aware, most of our village houses were reliant on 'privies' or ECs (earth closets) to dispose of their sewage. In times past it is possible that where there was a flowing ditch near to a house, Newnham people might have tipped their waste into it. Certainly, into the twentieth century privies, which could be rotated round the garden, were common and there may have been cesspits. About 1883, septic tanks were introduced into America and the concept spread so that thereafter the larger Newnham houses, and some of the newly built cottages, were equipped with septic tanks well into the twentieth century.

Where cottages relied on ECs, and also on well water for drinking water, there could be cross contamination. In 1948, the wells used by the residents of Green View and the Homestead (mentioned above) were found to be contaminated by various bacteria and the landlord was required to connect the premises reliant on these wells to the mains water supply.

In about 1971, a Borough Councillor living on The Green, getting fed up with the frequency with which his septic tank filled, usually with rainwater, decided to get Newnham put on main drains. This happened about 1977 but was not without its problems: Basingstoke Rural District Council (as it then was) chose the cheapest tender and, unsurprisingly, the company went bust. At some extra expense, the badly made manholes and the pipework, which had not been properly supported, were replaced. The whole process was, of course, a progressive move, but I believe it was the 'kiss of death' for the old Newnham. It meant that owners of tenanted cottages had, perforce, to connect them to the newly built main drains. In many cases they could not afford the cost, because the rents they were receiving were inadequate. If they had offset the cost by raising the rents, the cottagers could not have paid. So the landlords put the cottages on the market and the new owners set about improving their properties by connecting to the main drains. It also meant that anybody with spare land was tempted to develop it for speculative housing. Newnham was on the way to becoming a commuter village.

Today, almost every house in the village is connected to Thames Water's sewage treatment works at Hartley Wintney. There are several pumping stations within the civil parish: for example, at the Mobile Home Park at Water End, at the junction of Green Lane and Crown Lane, also close to the footbridge over the Newnham Brook on Church Path (and just within Kingsbridge Copse). There is also a major pumping station at the junction of Holt Lane and the A30, in Hook parish, which has sometimes failed and caused contamination of the River Whitewater.

Electricity

Currently it is unknown when electricity reached Newnham village, although it appears that electricity reached Newnham and Hook School in 1934. Before this, and early in the twentieth century, some of the larger houses chose to establish their own electricity plants. In the case of Newnham Hill, a shed was built about 1910 which contained a substantial engine driven by paraffin. Every Friday, this engine chugged away for about eight hours to charge the bank of some 20 accumulators; these provided a 12-volt DC supply to the house. On Friday, Saturday and Sunday evenings, the light in the house was good; on Monday, Tuesday and Wednesday, it was increasingly dimmer; by Thursday, the whole house was rather crepuscular; and on Friday, the cycle repeated. In 1943 Newnham Hill was at last connected to the mains electricity supply.

Gas

Although mains gas had reached Hook and probably Newnham's parish boundary in the 1930s, our village was not connected. In 1995–96, a parishioner wishing to switch to gas paid an exorbitant sum for the supply to be piped down Tylney Lane. Thereafter, for a much-reduced price, many houses chose to tap into the supply. Currently gas is available to every dwelling here, but sometimes Southern Gas can charge a ridiculously large sum to make the connection.

Telephone system

I believe the telephone exchange in Hook opened about 1925. When one consults *Kelly's Directory of Hampshire* (1927), it seems that fairly few private residences, and few business premises, in and around Hook had signed up to the telephone service. The first person to have a telephone locally was Mrs Cahen who lived on Scures Hill, approximately where 1, Baredown Close is today. The earliest Newnham household to join the service was the Old Rectory, now Newnham House, then occupied by Brigadier Sclater-Booth; its number was Hook 7. Another household, probably in the first wave of joining, was Newnham Green Farm, where Mrs F. E. W. Bell lived; it was Hook 92. However, not everybody was prepared to publicise their telephone number. For example, Mr W. M. C. Pechell joined the system early with the telephone number Hook 18, but remained ex-directory.

The first telephones round here were similar to the one in the image shown. To make a phone call, one lifted the earpiece and jiggled its cradle up and down to make contact with the operator at the exchange; she would connect one with the other number, but sometimes the operator would explain that it was pointless to try, because the person one wished to speak with was out or even away from home.

In due course, the Hook exchange was automated. During the 1970s all our telephone numbers had to have four figures beginning with 2 and followed by 4, 5 or 6 according to the choice of the householder. Single figure numbers such as Hook 7 became 2407, or 2507 or 2607; double figure numbers such as Hook 48 became 2448, or 2548 or 2648; triple figure numbers like Hook

125 became 2125. Then all Hook numbers were preceded by '76' for the Hook exchange. In April 1995, the STD code for Hook exchange was changed from 0256 to 01256, followed by a six-figure number beginning with 762.

Initially, most cottages were not connected to the exchange but to enable the residents to make calls there was a red telephone box on Newnham Green (**Fig. 31**) by the crossroads. It was available for anyone to use, provided that they had at least two old pennies[1] (2d) to make a local call. Later, British Telecom (BT) removed the red phone-box and replaced it with a largely glass structure. As time passed more and more houses in the village joined the exchange, and increasingly people owned mobile phones, so BT decided to remove the phone-box. Newnham Parish Council tried to prevent this development because the box was a feature on The Green; however, BT prevailed, chiefly because the box was vandalised. The box went in 2009.

High Speed Broadband

High Speed Broadband became available to Newnham houses on the west and north side of Newnham Road and Newnham Green in 2020. Then, after much effort by various villagers, it has become available, since late 2023, to nearly all the rest of the community.

Newnham Post Office (see also Chapter 5)

Already in 1898 Newnham had a Post Office[2], with Mrs Martha Lodge as sub-postmistress and shopkeeper; it was situated at the right-hand end of Crown Lodge, where there was a counter covered with oilcloth; and her daughter, Miss A. A. Lodge (Gussie Lodge), was the sub-postmistress in 1927[3], remaining in post until she died on 11 February 1965, aged 82. Then in the same year Mrs Isobel Gary re-opened Newnham's Post Office in Yew Tree Cottage on Newnham

1 Old pennies were the pre-decimalisation (before 1971) coins:
12d = 1 shilling, 20 shillings = 1 pound.

2 *Kelly's Directory of Hampshire and the Isle of Wight* (London: 1898), p. 235.

3 *Kelly's Directory of Hampshire and the Isle of Wight* (London: 1927), p. 302.

Road. Unfortunately, she had to discontinue the business for health reasons in 2003, and sadly she died on 15 December 2005.

Newnham's Post Office was in some ways akin to the bar at the Old House at Home, except that it was usually housewives who tarried to chat with Gussie, and later Isobel, and the other customers, exchanging village news and gossip and commenting on matters further afield. In contrast, the Old House at Home was where the men of the village discussed important matters of the day over their pints. Their womenfolk very seldom entered the pub, probably never unless accompanied by their husbands.

Carrier (see also Chapter 5)

Nowadays, with our ready access to motor cars, it is probably hard to believe that even as late as 1927 there was a Carrier operating in Newnham.[4] John Morris used to live on Newnham Green until about 1914 and he then moved house to the Barracks. He would take orders from householders in the village (and doubtless much further afield) to buy goods in Basingstoke (on Wednesdays and Saturdays) and Reading (on Tuesdays and Saturdays). I believe he had a horse and cart which would have enabled him to carry large items when necessary, and return them when they were unsuitable.

Home Delivery

Currently, largely as a result of Covid-19[5], many in Newnham have come to use home deliveries for any- and every-thing, a practice that was not often employed, at least for food, before 2019. Today all supermarkets (e.g. ASDA, Co-op, Morrisons, Ocado, Sainsbury's, Tesco and Waitrose) respond to customers' orders by bringing the chosen goods to one's door in dedicated refrigerated vans.

4 *Kelly's Directory of Hampshire and the Isle of Wight* (1927), *op. cit.*, p. 302.

5 Covid-19 is a widely-spread contagious disease caused by the coronavirus SARS-CoV-2. To help control its spread, the Government required people to stay close to their homes. Generally, only food shops and pharmacies remained open and to maintain sales, supermarkets and other shops introduced home deliveries.

Bus Services

I recall that during WW2 there used to be a regular bus service through the middle of Newnham that came from Basingstoke and went on to Rotherwick, Mattingley, Heckfield and Reading on Wednesdays and Saturdays. The bus to Reading came early and returned about an hour later, and a second Reading bus came from Basingstoke during the afternoon and returned similarly. The service enabled one to do some rather focused shopping at either end before returning home the same day. It has long since been discontinued.

Currently, there is a Stagecoach No. 13 service between Basingstoke and Bordon, along the A30 to Hook, and thence to Odiham and Alton about once an hour between 6.10 a.m. and 8 p.m. There is a bus stop at the bottom of Crown Lane and another adjacent to the Hogget on Hook Common. The service runs in reverse from about 6.15 a.m. until 8 p.m. on weekdays, with a modified service on Saturdays.[6]

Medical Services

The foregoing services meet daily needs to enable a reasonably comfortable day-to-day existence. Medical services are of a different kind, in that they focus on sickness.

Perhaps back in mediaeval times, there was someone in the village who might have been called a nurse. She – probably it was usually a lady – would have applied 'natural' remedies based on extracts from plants to treat specific ailments; for example, the bark of willow trees contains salicylic acid, the active ingredient in aspirin. She might also have sat up with the dying, and after death would have 'laid out' the dead person. From the eighteenth century comes an example from the overseers' book: 'Dame Pointer' was paid 3s. 6d. in March 1796 for 'setting up with Pole Coston' (Polly, or Mary, Cawson was buried on 22 February 1796).[7] When a doctor was required, Newnham looked to Odiham, as was recorded in 1795: 'John Harris, surgeon of Odiham agreed to take the parish business [...] by the year for £4. 4. 0, including everything except

6 Stagecoach internet timetable.

7 Hampshire Record Office 67M80A, PO1 (11 March 1796) and 67M80A, PR1.

the smallpox.'[8] And when smallpox struck, as it appears to have done from time to time, Mr Covey of Basingstoke was called on; for example, 'March 21, 1799, [...] paid Mr Covey for Welch and his wife with smallpox £3. 3. 0.'[9]

The role of laying out bodies occasionally continued in the village into the early twentieth century. A much-loved lady with this role was Mrs Miriam Poulter, who died on 23 December 1909, and whose gravestone in Newnham churchyard was 'erected by her many friends' in the community.

8 Hampshire Record Office 67M80A, PO1 (5 April 1795) and *Universal British Directory of Trade, Commerce and Manufacture*, Vol. II (1793), p. 167 ('John Harris, Surgeon, Odiham').

9 Hampshire Record Office 67M80A, PO1 (21 March 1799) and *Universal British Directory of Trade, Commerce and Manufacture*, *op.cit.*, p. 317 ('John Covey, Apothecary, Basingstoke; Charles Covey, Surgeon, Basingstoke.').

APPENDICES

APPENDIX 1
Map 1, Gough Map, 1325–1350

This is a section of the Ordnance Survey facsimile published in 1935. It is named after Richard Gough, who bequeathed the map to the Bodleian Library, Oxford University, in 1809.

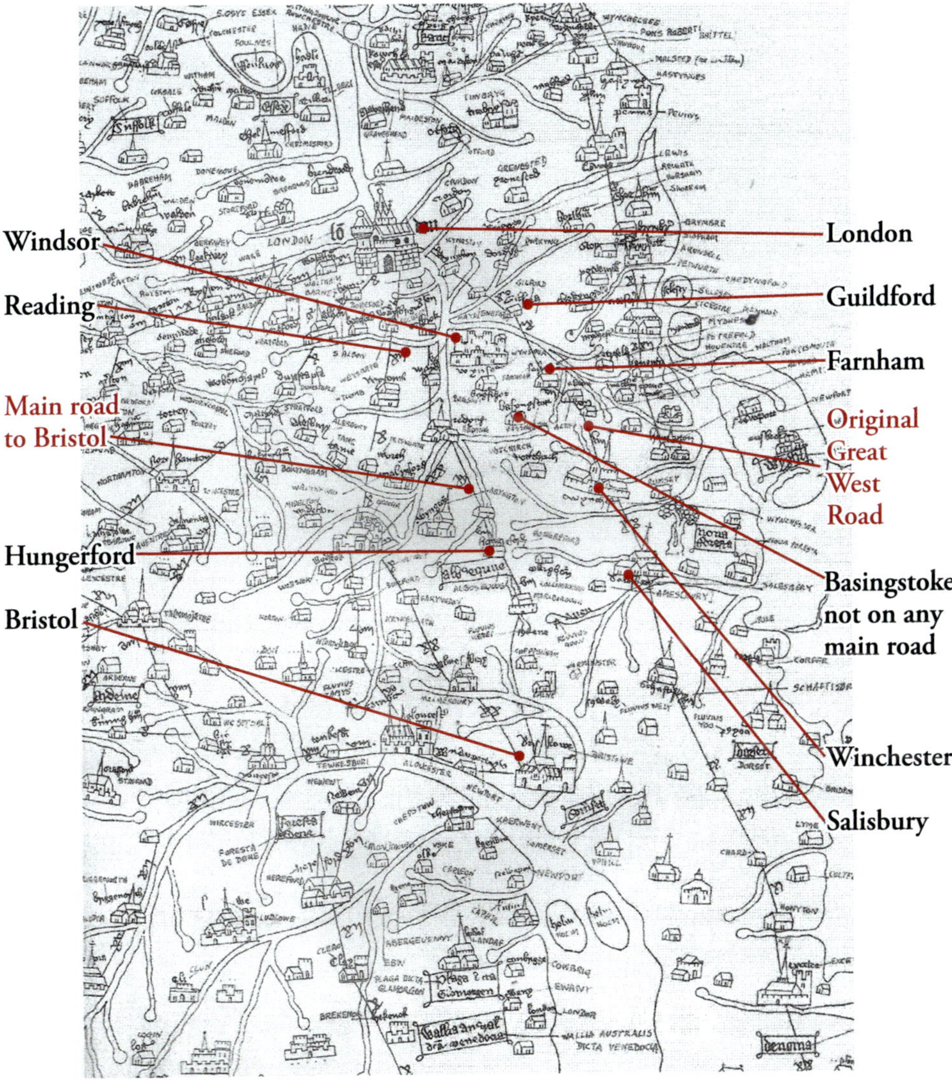

The Gough Map shows the chief towns. The unbroken (semi-straight) lines are the main roads. The Bristol road is almost the modern A4. Rivers are shown as double lines.

Map 2, Winchester College Map, *c.*1552

A sixteenth-century pictorial 'map' of Hook dated about 1552, showing land more or less opposite Old Raven House and on the south of the present A30.

This perspective was prepared for Winchester College and is used by kind permission of The Warden and Fellows. It was painted about 1552 to help explain a dispute between John Hooker of Hook and the tenant, John Jakes, of the College's property, Hurstland, in Hook. The reason for including it here is to show that the main road through Hook (then part of Newnham) was called 'The hy way ledyng from London to Basyngstoke'. It also gives some indication of the kind of traffic using this road.

Hurst Barn is shown close to the gate at the lower right of the perspective. It is still there today, having been converted into a house.

Map 3, Thomas Langdon Map, 1616

Showing the landholdings in Newnham, Owen's Farm and surroundings, held by Corpus Christi College, Oxford (Ref: CCC MS 533/II f.), reproduced here by kind permission of the President and Fellows of Corpus Christi College, Oxford.

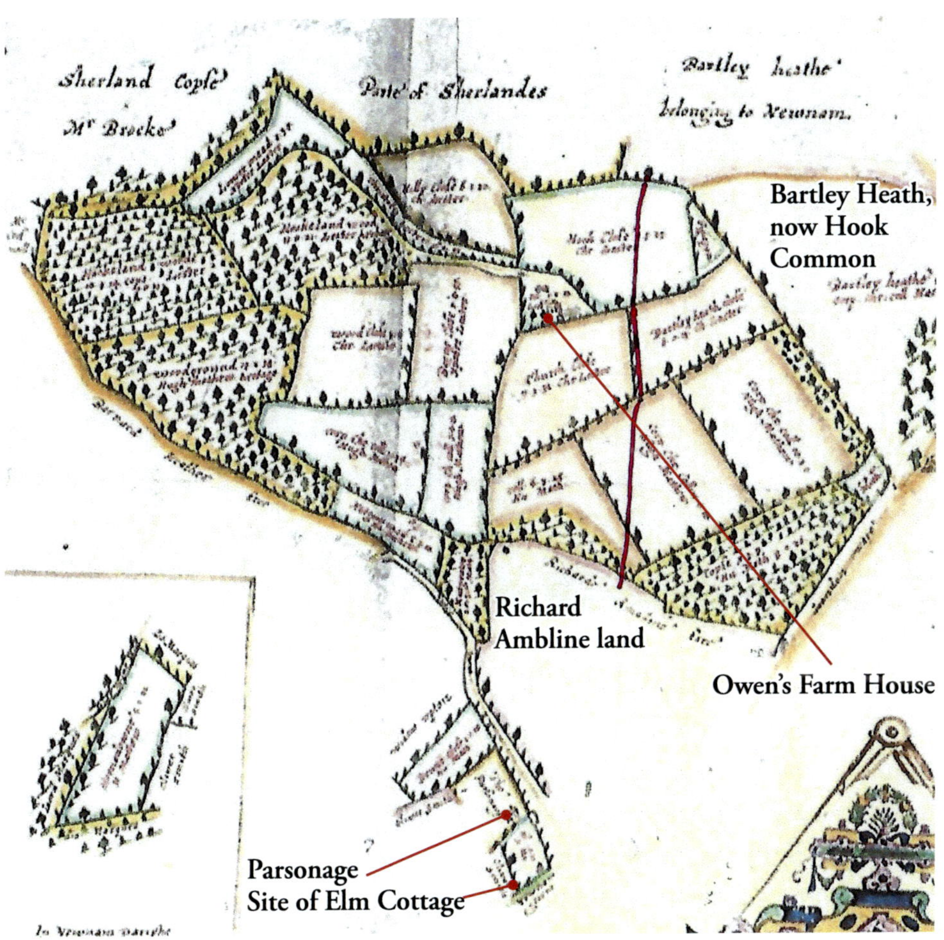

Map 4, John Ogilby's Road Map, 1675

A detail showing part of the London to Land's End road.

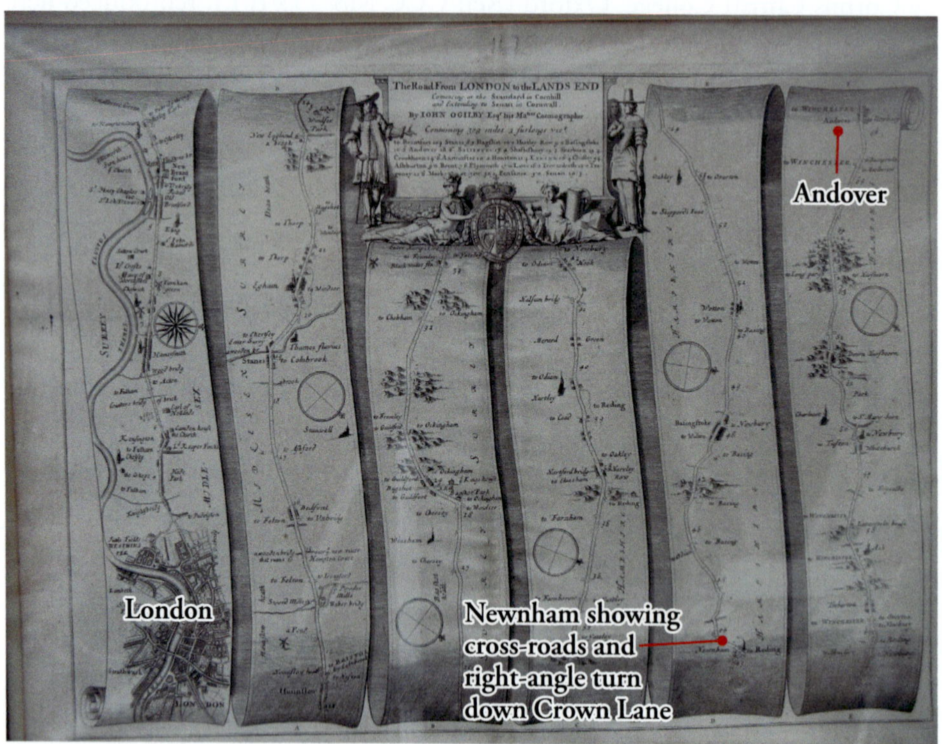

John Ogilby (1600–1676) was a Scottish publisher and cartographer, best known for his road atlas named *Britannia*, published in 1675, which depicted in strip form most of the major routes in England and Wales. The roads were measured using a surveyor's wheel, and were plotted on the scale of one inch to the statute mile (1:63,360), which was Ogilby's own innovation. These are marked and numbered on each map, the miles being further divided into furlongs. At that period, the measurement of many minor roads had used a locally defined mile, rather than the standard mile of 1,760 standard yards which Ogilby adopted in his atlas, thus setting the standard for road maps in future.

The significance of the illustrated map is that it shows that the Great West Road was routed through Newnham in 1675 (as it had been since approximately 1400). By 1786 it had been re-routed away from Newnham and over Scures Hill, effectively the current A30.

Map 5, Map Of Newnham, *c.*1700

This early eighteenth-century map of Newnham, held by Hampshire Record Office (33M71), is in poor condition.

Map 6, Tylney Estate Map Of 1774

A detail showing Newnham Green.
The original large map is held by Hampshire Record Office, Ref. 10M48.
[Note: Newnham Green Farm is omitted from this map.]

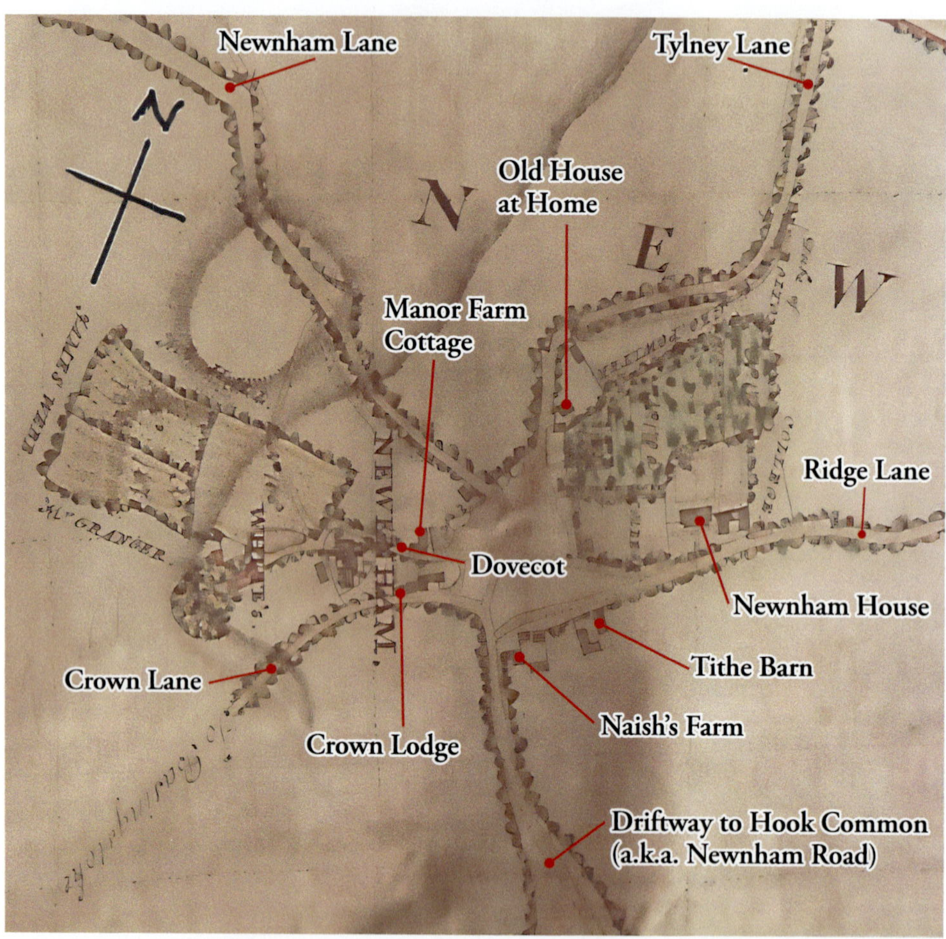

Map 7, Newnham Tithe Map 1842 (central section)

This map is held by Hampshire Record Office, Ref. 67M80.

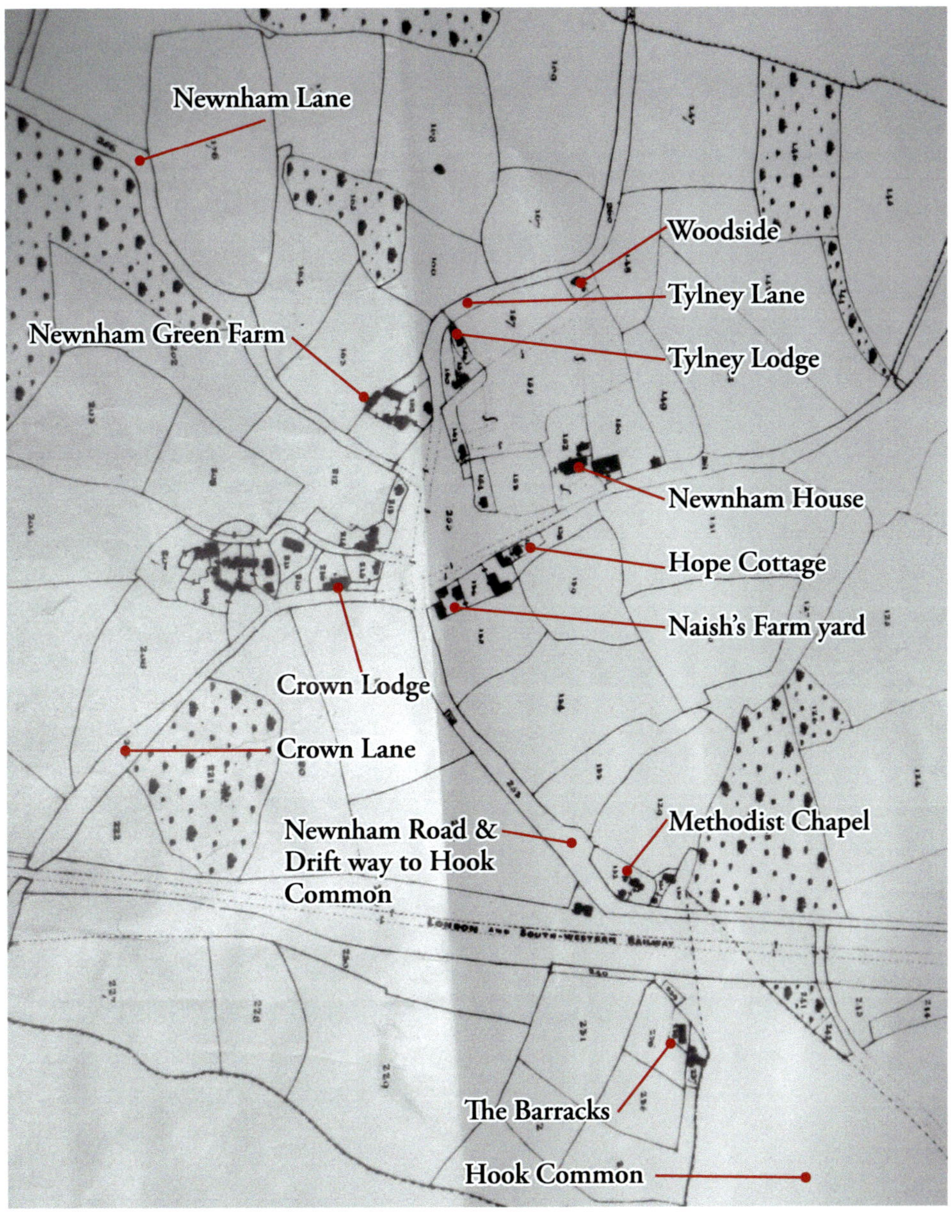

Map 8, Ordnance Survey Map, 1877

1877 O.S. 6 inch map. Courtesy of Hampshire Cultural Trust

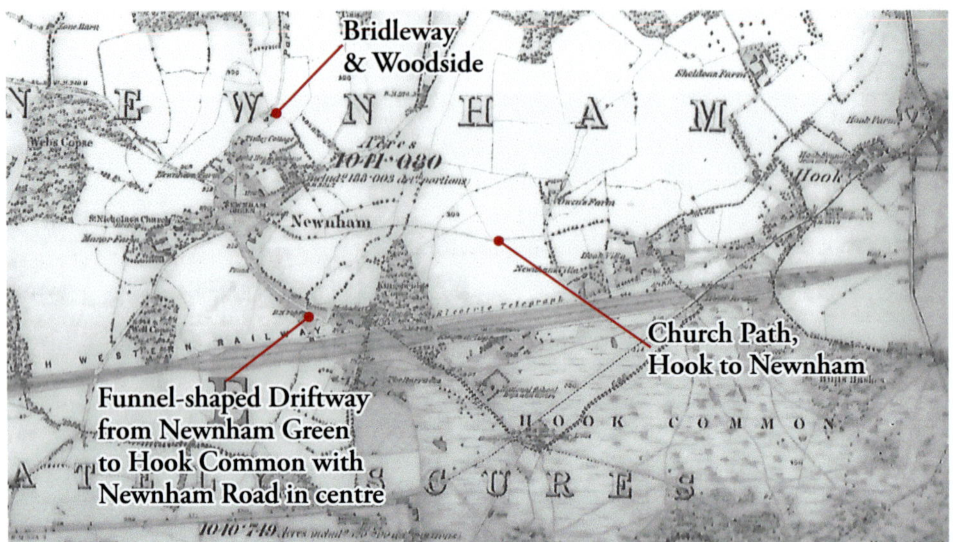

Map 9, Ordnance Survey Map, 1881

A detail showing Newnham Green (Scale: 25 inches to 1 mile).
This map reveals the relatively restricted area of housing at that date. There were, then, no dwellings along Newnham Road until the Methodist Chapel and then Thorn Cottage (a.k.a. Valentine Cottage).

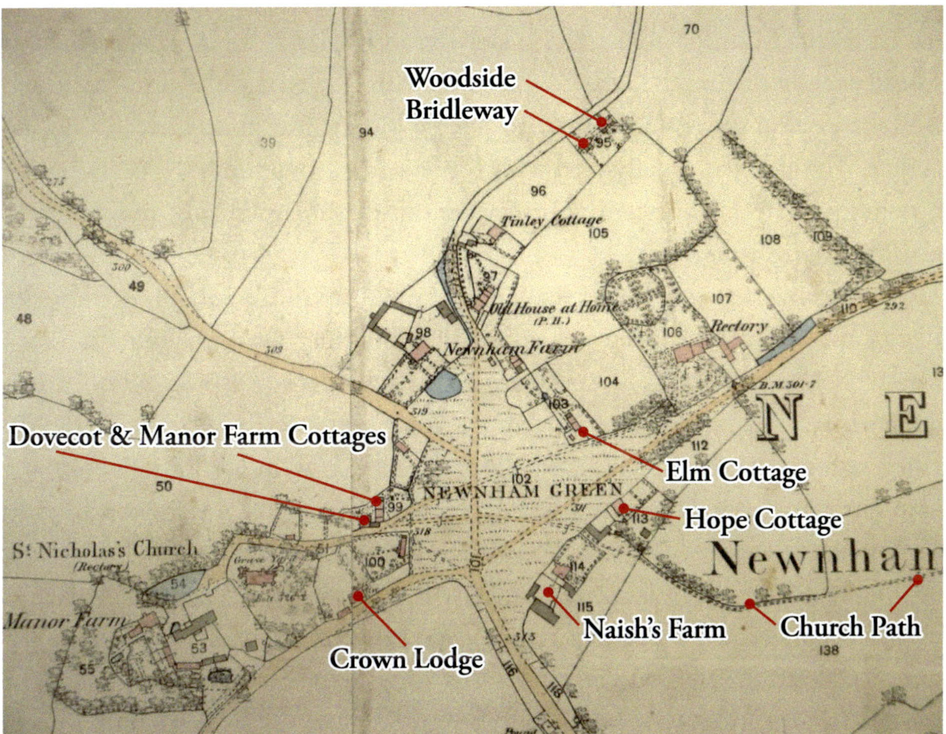

APPENDIX 2
The Black Death (1)

In 1999, I made a study of how the Black Death affected 30 local villages for the Hook Local History Society's Millennium Exhibition. What follows is an edited version for *Newnham, our Newnham.*

The Black Death is the name given to a devastating outbreak of plague which reached Europe about 1347, arriving in England in June 1348 where it spread rapidly during the next two to three years. The bacterial disease, caused by *Yersinia pestis,* was transmitted to people by rat fleas and between infected people. The afflicted usually died within a few days, sometimes within hours, of becoming ill. In the fourteenth century the causes were unknown, and there was no effective treatment.

We know that the disease had a direct effect upon Newnham, because the Rector died. However, I have to admit that anything I write about the Black Death locally is, inevitably, speculation because there seems to be no direct documentary evidence, such as Manor Court rolls, relating to any of the 30 villages around Hook which I studied for the Millennium Exhibition.

For Hampshire as a whole, the Register of Bishop William Edington (Bishop of Winchester between 1346 and 1366)[1] provides good data about all the clergy appointments for the Winchester Diocese. By studying this Register for villages within 7½ miles of present-day Hook it has been possible to discover how the disease affected the clergy. In an attempt to discover the normal mortality rate for the local clergy, an analysis was undertaken of clergy vacancies and appointments during the whole of Bishop Edington's time. The study covered 30 parishes and two monastic houses[2], all within Winchester diocese; some present-day villages do

1 Dom S. F. Hickey (ed.), *The Register of William Edington, Bishop of Winchester 1346–1366* (2 vols., Hampshire Record Office for Hampshire County Council, 1986 Part 1 and 1987 Part 2).

2 Parishes: Basingstoke/Old Basing, Bramley, Cliddesden, Crondall, Dogmersfield, Eastrop, Ellisfield, Eversley, Farleigh Wallop, Froyle, Hartley Wespall, Hartley Wintney, Heckfield, Herriard, Mapledurwell, Monk Sherborne, Nately Scures, Newnham, Oakley, Odiham, Sherborne St. John, Silchester, South Warnborough, Stratfield Saye, Stratfield Turgis, Tunworth, Weston Corbett, Winchfield, Winslade, Worting. A table showing the vacancies in each of these parishes is given in Table 2.
Religious houses: Pamber Priory and Wintney Abbey. This is probably unrepresentative because the Bishop seems only to have been concerned about the fitness of the head of each institution. In fact, the Prior at Pamber and the Abbess at Wintney Abbey both died in 1349. These two deaths have been omitted from this study.

Table 1

Black Death: Mortality Rates for Clergy within 7½ miles of Hook

Year		Deaths	Year		Deaths
1346	Normal year	0	1357	Normal year	1
1347	Normal year	0	1358	Normal year	0
1348	Normal year	1	1359	Normal year	0
1349	Exceptional year	31	1360	Normal year	1
1350	Exceptional year	3	1361	Exceptional year	19
1351	Exceptional year	7	1362	Exceptional year	4
1352	Normal year	0	1363	Normal year	1
1353	Normal year	3	1364	Normal year	0
1354	Normal year	0	1365	Normal year	0
1355	Normal year	1	1366	Normal year	1
1356	Normal year	0			

In summary, nine deaths during the 16 'normal years' or about one every other year on average. During the first 'exceptional years' (1349–1351), there were 41 deaths; of these it seems reasonable to suggest that two might have occurred for normal (non-plague) reasons, such as typhoid, or old age. Thus, the Black Death of 1349–1351 would seem to have killed some 39 clergy. During the outbreak in 1361–1362, 29 clergy died of which perhaps one was due to natural causes.

Table 2, which can be seen in Appendix 2 (2), gives more details, parish by parish.

not feature because they seem not to have had their own incumbents in the mid 1300s. This analysis of all clergy appointments (see Table 1) indicates that one rector or vicar died, or was replaced, on average, every other year in normal times.

'The plague struck the diocese of Winchester with special violence; 48.8% of all beneficed clergy died [...] the register demonstrates how many benefices had to be filled.'[3] The statistics in Table 1 speak for themselves.

To try and estimate how the general population was affected, I have assumed death rates among the clergy, due to the plague, were broadly paralleled in the rest of the population. The turnover in local clergy during the Black Death provides a shattering indication of how the disease affected North-East Hampshire.

3 *Registers of Bishop Edington*, *op. cit.*, p. xii.

As regards the Hook neighbourhood, during 1346, 1347 and 1348, the three years immediately before the disease struck, the death of just one parson was recorded from near Hook; this suggests an average of one or two deaths every three years presumably from 'natural causes'. Then the picture changes dramatically, because very late in 1348 or early in 1349 this dreadful affliction struck. In March 1349 alone, four new vicars or rectors were appointed, another one in April, four more in May and the dismal story continued to unfold. In all, 25 new clergy were installed during the year, with three added early in 1350, and five more in 1351. It would seem the peak was during January to August 1349, but deaths among the clergy rumbled on for about another two years. It is arguable that some of the new men 'in post' during 1351 were replacing victims of other diseases, but as the Black Death did not die out after its first strike, it was probably the direct or indirect cause of some deaths in 1351.

The 30 local villages are assumed to have had one member of the clergy each at the beginning of the Pestilence. Twelve new clergy were replaced in villages which lost two or more parsons during the 1349–1351 period, making a total of 42 clergy 'in post' during the whole period. Of these ecclesiastics, 40 died; but if the normal death rate could have been expected to be two during these years, then it seems that 38 may have died as a result of the Black Death in North-East Hampshire. It would be spurious to claim any precision in this figure, but as an indication of the impact of the disease it is very telling.

One writer alive at the time, John of Fordun (writing of Scotland) states, 'this [*the disease*] attacked especially the meaner sort and common people'.[4] And in some places it was said 'the young died in greater proportion than the old'.[5] The clergy were likely to have been better fed and housed than many of the population and they were certainly in an older age bracket than 'the young'; this may indicate that although their death rate was perhaps higher than the average, proportionately the clergy may not have died to a much greater extent than their fellows in the wider community. If that were to have been the case the local population must have been shattered.

There is no direct evidence for the villages around Hook, but it seems possible that between 1349 and 1351 up to two-thirds of the population may have died in some places, although the figure which has been proposed for most

4 Quoted in Philip Ziegler, *The Black Death* (Collins, 1969), p. 199.

5 Barbara W. Tuchman, *A Distant Mirror: The Calamitous 14th Century* (Macmillan, 1979), p. 98.

of Britain (i.e. not just for Hampshire) is between 23 per cent and 45 per cent: 'a halfway point between [...] would suggest a death rate of roughly a third'.[6]

Ten years later the disease struck again. 'The second epidemic of 1361, by any standards other than those of the earlier outbreak, was catastrophic in its dimensions'.[7] In these same 30 parishes around Hook, 11 clergy died in that year, and eight more died in 1362. Perhaps they did not all die from *Yersinia pestis*, but it seems likely to have been the main cause. Thus, 19 priests died out of 32 (because in Farleigh Wallop, two died in quick succession): that is to say, 59 per cent. What happened to the ordinary people is unknown; many may have been young and perhaps more susceptible than the adults who had survived the earlier visitation. The older inhabitants surely felt they had seen it all before.

6 Ziegler, *op. cit.*, p. 230.

7 *Ibid*, p. 234.

Table 2

Black Death Statistics Analysed F

Parish	1346	1347	1348	1349
Basing/Basingstoke				v. vacant 3/6
Bramley				
Cliddesden			r. resig. 23/4 r. exch. 16/12	r. vacant D 22/3 r. vacant 18/9
Crondall R&V				v. vacant D 7/3
Dogmersfield	vacant 18/5 vacant 21/7			
Eastrop				
Ellisfield				r. vacant
Eversley			r. exch. 13/6	
Farleigh Wallop			r. exch. 9/2 r. vacant 29/4	r. vacant 19/8
Froyle R&V		r. 'lapse' 29/1		v. vacant 13/5 r. exch. 17/7 r. exch. 9/10
Hartley Wespall				r. vacant 28/3 r. vacant 2/7 r. vacant 17/10
Hartley Wintney R&V				r. vacant 5/5 v. 8/8 r. vacant 10/12
Heckfield				v. vacant 9/5
Herriard				v. vacant 7/6
Mapledurwell (Chantry)		resig. 6/3		
Monk Sherborne				v. vacant D 11/3
Nately Scures				r. vacant 22/5
Newnham				r. vacant 18/8
Oakley				vacant 17/6
Odiham		v. 30/1		v. vacant 13/6 v. vacant 14/7
Sherborne St John R&V				v. vacant 7/5 v. vacant 24/5 r. vacant D 13/10
Silchester				r. vacant 29/5
South Warnborough				
Stratfield Saye				
Stratfield Turgis			vacant D 23/9	
Tunworth			r. resig. 16/4	r. vacant D 6/3 r. vacant 22/11
Weston Corbett				
Winchfield				
Winslade				vacant 31/3 r. vacant 6/8
Worting				r. exch. 10/1
Exceptional year deaths				32
Number of villages where at least one incumbent died in an exceptional year				20

NOTES r. or R = rector V = vicar D = died
exch. = an exchange of benefice between two incumbents
resig. or res. = resigned vacant or vac. = the previous incumbent had left.

he Parishes Within 7.5 Miles Of Hook

1350	1351	1352	1361	1362	1363
	v. vacant 3/9		v. vacant 25/10		
			v. vacant 30/10		
	r. vacant 24/10		vacant D 18/8		
		r. exch. 11/7	v. vacant D 18/8		
			r. vacant D 3/9		
			r. resig. 20/11		
	vacant 3/6		r. vacant D 18/9		
				vac. 'lapse' 18/9	
r. vacant 26/4					
		r. vacant 24/9			
			r. vacant 22/10		
			v. vacant 22/10		
	r. exch. 9/10				
			r. vacant 4/10		
	v. vac 8/11[not death]	v. resig. 10/10	v. vacant 21/8		
			r. vacant 3/9		
	v. vacant 4/2			v. 16/6	v. resig. 9/7
				r. vacant 23/8	
	r. vacant 18/4		r. vacant 22/10		
			v. vacant 24/7		
			v. vacant 26/10	v. vacant 19/1	
		r. exch. 17/6		v. vacant 11/12	
r. vacant 31/1			r. vacant 27/7		
			r. vacant 14/10		
			r. vacant 5/11		
		r. vacant 14/4			r. vac. 'lapse
r. vacant 'lapse' 22/5					
			r. vacant 7/12		
r. resig. 5/1		r. ?resig. 17/9	r. resig. 6/5	r. res. 29/7	
3	6		19	5	
3	6		15	5	

After mid-March 1349 the death of the former incumbent, as the reason for the vacancy, is not usually mentioned: the Register only states 'vacant'. 'lapse' is used in the Register presumably to show that the possessor of the advowson had not presented a new parson and the Bishop had therefore put in his own nominee.

APPENDIX 3

Church Documents (1)

Extracts from publications by Sir William Dugdale

For further details pertaining to the establishment of Pamber Priory (see Chapter 6), extracts from the twelfth-century charters of Henry de Port and his presumed kin, John de Port and Adam de Port, together with other related information, are reproduced below. These extracts are taken from two publications by the seventeenth-century antiquarian and herald, Sir William Dugdale: *Monasticon Anglicanum*[1] (originally written in Latin) and *The Baronage of England.*[2]

From William Dugdale, *Monasticon Anglicanum*[3]

Referring to the Priory of Monk Sherborne, or West Shirburne as it was then known:

'Here, says Tanner, was an Alien Priory of Benedictine Monks, dedicated to St Mary and St John, Cell to the Abbey of St Vigor at Cerasy [*Cerisy*] in Normandy, to which it was given by Henry de Port, one of the Barons of the Exchequer, *temp* Hen. I [...] It was afterwards restored to the Hospital [*of St Julian*] at Southampton, and is enjoyed by the Provost and Fellows of Queen's College in Oxford, as Masters of that Hospital.'

NUMBER I

Carta Henrici de Portu, Fundatoris (Charter of Henry du Port)

'[...] *Ecclesiam de Neoham cum decima ipsius villae tota, et cum decima virgulti*[4],

1 Sir William Dugdale (1605–1686) was an English antiquary and herald, whose scholarly researches and publications were influential in the development of medieval history as an academic subject. His study of the history of English religious houses, *Monasticon Anglicanum, or, the History of the Ancient Abbies, and other Monasteries, Hospitals, Cathedrals and Collegiate Churches, in England and Wales. With divers French, Irish and Scotch Monasteries formerly relating to England*, was published in three volumes between 1655 and 1673, and translated into English from the original Latin in an abridged edition in 1693.

2 William Dugdale, *The Baronage of England, or, An historical account of the lives and most memorable actions of our English nobility in the Saxons time to the Norman conquest, and from thence, of those who had their rise before the end of King Henry the Third's reign deduced from publick records, antient historians, and other authorities*. It was published in 1675–76.

3 The quoted extracts from *Monasticon Anglicanum* are from Vol. VI, part 2, of the 1849 edition, pp. 1013–14.

4 The Latin word *Virgultum* (plural *virgulti*) translates as a thicket, copse or brushwood, which may refer to the commons or common woodlands of Newnham.

et cum decima duorum molendinorum, et cum una virgata terrae, et altera virgata ad Mappedreuuellam.'

The above Latin text may be translated as:
The church of Newnham with all the tithes of the same, and with the tithes of the woodland, and with the tithes of two mills, and with one virgate (c. 30 acres) of land, and another virgate in Mapledurwell.

[the first nine of 20 signatories:]
Henricus de Portu
Hadvis uxor ejus
Guillielmus et Johannes filii ejus
Herbertus presbiter
Ulricus capellanus
Galfridus presbiter
Rogerius de Scuris [Roger de Scures[5]]
Henricus de Braibove, etc.

NUMBER II

Carta de Johannis de Port (Charter of John du Port)

'[...] *quinque didas terrae in Sipford quas Adhewisa mater mea* [...]', which may be translated as 'I give five [?virgates] of land in Sipford which my mother Adwise [...]'

There are no references to Newnham nor to Mapledurwell in this charter, but among the 27 witnesses are the following names:
Matildis uxor mea
Adam [et] *Hugo filii mei*
Reginaldus de Port
Henricus de Port
Matheus de Scures
Willielmus filius Adae [as this means 'Adam's son', it may refer to the above-named Adam]

5 Roger de Scures was probably lord of the Manor of Nately Scures, which formed part of the Hampshire possessions of Hugh de Port, remaining with his descendants until the early seventeenth century. (Information from website of St Swithun, Nately Scures.)

Willielmus filius Rogeri [probably Roger de Scures' son]
Rodbertus de Port
Hugo de Braibuf
Rodbertus de Port clericus et Johannes frater ejus

NUMBER III

Carta Adae de Port (Charter of Adam de Port)

This document includes the following statement which seems to confirm that Adam de Port was grandson to Henricus (see NUM. I): '[…] *quod Henricus de Port, avus meus, dedit eis* […]'

There are no references to Newnham nor Mapledurwell, but among the 14 witnesses are:

Sibilla comitissa uxore mea
Roberto de sancto Manuet
Hugone de Arundell
Matheo de Scures

NUMBER IV

Carta Willielmi de Sancto Johanne (Charter of William de Port[6])

This document includes a statement which seems to confirm that the subject of the charter was the son of Adam (see NUMBER III above): '[…] *ego Willielmus de Sancto Johanne, filius et haeres Adae de Port* […]'

There are no references to Newnham nor Mapledurwell, but among the 14 witnesses are:

Galfrido de sancto Johanne
Robert et Ada filiis meis
Roberto de Arundell

From William Dugdale, *The Baronage of England*[7]

'At the time of the General Survey, made by King William the Conqueror, Hugh de Port held fifty five Lordships of the King in Hantshire [*sic*]; whereof Basing was one, which became the Head of his Barony […]

6 William de Port changed his name to St John, which was a family surname on his mother's side of the family.

7 The quoted extracts from *The Baronage of England* are from Tome I of the original 1675 edition, pp. 463–4 (studied by the author in the Bodleian Library, University of Oxford, 28 July 1999).

'To whom succeeded Henry, his Son and Heir, who gave a great part of his Lordship of Shireburne (near Basing) to the Monks of St Vigor, at Cerasie in Normandy [...] and bequeathed his body to be there buried (viz at Cerasie) Hadwise his wife, with William and John his sons assenting thereto. About this time also, Adam de Port (Brother as I guess, to this Henry) gave[8] to those Monks of St Vigor, at Cerasie, the Chappel of Newnham, with all the Tithes of Mapeth and Welle, with one Yardland in Mapeth, and half a Yardland in Newnham, in the presence of William Giffard, then Bishop of Winchester, upon the day of the Dedication of that Chappel.

'Which Henry left issue John his Son and Heir who confirming the Grant of his Father to those monks then settled at Shireburne amongst other particulars, further bestowed on them the Chappel of St. Michael, with the Land of the old Castle of Basing; Maud his wife, with Adam and Hugh, his Sons, being witness thereto [...]

'This John, in 12 Hen 2 [*i.e. 1166*] upon the Assessment of Aid, for marrying the Kings Daughter certified the Knights Fees he then held, to be in number fifty five *De Veteri Feoffamento,* and two *De Novo*; for all which in 14 Hen 2 [*i.e. 1168*] he paid fifty seven marks.

'To him Succeeded Adam de Port, his eldest Son, who gave unto those Monks of Shireburne the whole Tithe of all his Mills there, in exchange for a Mill which they also had in Shireburne where at that time a Pool was; which Pool Henry de Port, his Grandfather, bestowed on them at the first Foundation of that Monastery; the Countess Sybilla, his Wife, witnessing the grant.'

8 *Ex Autog. Penès Praepos & Scholares Coll. Reginalis Oxon.*

Church Documents (2)

Newnham Clergy, an historical record

1304–1305	William de Essex
1304–1306	Andrew de Guldeford (Deacon)
1311	Robert de Kelkefeld
1314–1326	Andrew de Guldeford
1326–1337	Thomas de Menestoke
1337	Walter de Heyford
1339	John de Peuseye
1339	Walter de Stratford
1339	Henry de Twyverton (Clerk)
1349	William de Ranby (Clerk)
?–1378	William de Rovenby
1378	William de Wynton
1381	William Wychot (or Withot) Parson of St Peter's, without Southgate, Winchester
1389	William Bereford
1408	John Stockton (Clerk)
1427	John Fereby (Rector)
(Records lost for intervening years up to 1449)	
1449–1477	William Belne
1477–1507	Thomas Cuthbertson
1507	Edward Hylton
1507–1519	William Eastwood, BA
1528–1521	Richard Fetherstone, MA
1521–1534	Robert Preston, MA
1534–1538	Edward Lush (or Loyshe), BD, Canon of Carlisle, 1542
*c.*1552–1553	Thomas Peyrson
1567	Nicolas Cooke, MA
1589	John Hewlett, BA (Clerk)
1589	Nicolas Smith (his will is dated 5/11/1617)
1618	William Cape
1654	James Potter
1658	Andrew Whelpdale (also Rector of Dogmersfield from 1671)
1679	Philip Nanson (also Rector of Dogmersfield from 1679)
1719–1740	Michael Hutchinson, DD[1]

1 Also Minister of Hammersmith (1712), Rector of Longdon (1721) and Freford (1727).

1741–1761	Robert Atkinson, MA
1761–1816	Joseph Richmond, DD (died 3/1/1816 aged 98)
1816–1844	Richard Hunter, MA
1845–1879	George Wylie, MA
1879–1889	Andrew Wallace Milroy, MA
1889–1899	Paul Daniel Eyre, DD
1901–1916	Charles Henry Coryndon Baker, DD
1916–1924	William Hipwood Mowatt, MA
1924–1933	Edward Waring Ormerod
1933–1944	Horace Spence Footman, MA
1945–1950	Frederick Alexander Saunders
1951–1955	Roy Aubrey Dacre, BD
1955–1961	Kenneth Caesar Davis
1961–1963	Bernard Williamson, BA
1964–1980	Reginald Haines
1981–1986	Brian Cowell
1986–1997	Michael Hawes, AKC
1999–2011	Michael Richard Moore Jaggs, NSM
2008–2016	Jane Leese, NSM
2014–2021	Linda Scard, NSM
2018–2021	Helen O'Sullivan, Curate
2021–	Deborah Veel

This list, updated to the present day, is largely based on information gathered by J. R. Magrath (1839–1930), Provost of Queen's College, Oxford. Magrath had studied the biographies because Queen's held the Newnham advowson (the right to present clergy to the Newnham benefice), after about 1452. Thereafter, and in certain cases, e.g. Edward Hylton, from as early as 1507, the Rectors were presented by Queen's and in many cases came from Cumberland, or Westmorland, because Queen's was a foundation for men from the North-West.

The arrangement whereby Queen's nominated one of its Fellows to be Rector of Newnham (and Mapledurwell) ceased after 1900. However, the advowson remains with the College, although now shared with the Bishop of Winchester, who possesses the advowsons of Nately Scures, Up Nately and Greywell. Since 1982, these five villages have been together as one United Parish.

Church Documents (3)

List of Persons Responsible for the Upkeep of the Churchyard Fence between 1766 and 1835[1]

No	Feet & inches	Panels	1766	1782–86	1796/ 1812–16	1816–35
1	29'	3	Alexander Wix	Clue	Jn. Rogers	Jn. Rogers
2	28'	4	Edmund Chamberlain, Paper Mill	Chamberlen	Thos. Horn	Ed.Chamberlin
3	15' 8"	2	James Webb	Webb	J. Horn	Jn. Webb
4	10' 10"	1	George Poulter	Polter	Ben Poulter	Mr. Cooper
5	11' 6"	2	James Webb	Webb	Mrs Bird	Jn. White
6	26' 6"	3	Rush Mason	Mason	Rev. Langdon	Rev. Davis
7	26'	3	Charles Roberson, Sheldons	Stevens	J. W. Clark	Rev. Parker
8	17'	2	William Naish	Naish	Rowland	?
9	9'	1	Norman, The Shop	Norman	Varndell	?Baldock
10	12' 6"	2	John Keep	Bath Jnr	Hockley	?Bartlett
11	11'	1 + gate	Rev Dr Richmond	Richmond	n/a	Mr Hunter, Rector
12	30'	4	James Webb	Webb	n/a	Mrs Hewett
13	15'	2	John Stevens, Tichenors	Chamberlen	J. Horn	Ed.Chamberlin
14	24'	3	Thomas King	King	J. W. Clark	Mr Luff
15	28' 6"	4	John Stevens, Hook Farm	Stevens	J. W. Clark	Mr Luff
16	31' 6"	4	Bernard Lee	Lee	John & James	Rogers
17	10' 4"	1	Thos. Balding, The Raven	Bullock	J. Hewett	Eli Lee
18	8'	1	John Newell	Lambel	J. Harris	Silvester
19	14'	2	Marshall, Crooked Billet	Chamberlen	n/a	?Dorchester
20	25'	3	Richard Baffe	Bath	n/a	Baffe
21	18'	2	David Crimble, Lyde Mill	Kite	n/a	Readman
22	16'	1+ gate	Earl Tylney, Malt House	Bath	Rogers	Mr Ellis

A picture of the fencing panels referred to may be seen in the 1832 illustration of Newnham's church, **Fig. 16.**

1 Hampshire Record Office: 67M80 PW1 & PO1.

APPENDIX 4
Wildlife In Newnham (1)

A List of Newnham Flora

This list is undoubtedly very far from complete. As far as possible I have tried to avoid reference to 'exotic' species in people's gardens, but of those which have escaped and become naturalised, to be found on waysides and verges, these get a mention. A question mark before or after the name signifies the author's uncertainty over identification.

The order in which the various species are recorded below follows that given in *Collins Flower Guide* (2010) and the English and scientific names here used are those given in the same book.

Ferns

Field Horsetail	*Equisetum arvense*
Bracken	*Pteridium aquilinum*
Hart's-tongue	*Phyllitis scolopendrium*
Wall Rue	*Asplenium ruta-muraria*
Male-fern	*Dryopteris filix-mas*
Conifers	
European Larch	*Larix decidua*
Scots Pine	*Pinus sylvestris*
Austrian Pine	*Pinus nigra*
Yew	*Taxus baccata*

Flowering Plants

Marsh Marigold	*Caltha palustris*
Winter Aconite	*Eranthis hyemalis*
Wood Anemone	*Anemone nemorosa*
Old Man's Beard	*Clematis vitalba*
Common Meadow Buttercup	*Ranunculus acris*
Creeping Buttercup	*Ranunculus repens*
Bulbous Buttercup	*Ranunculus bulbosus*
Goldilocks	*Ranunculus auricomus*
Celery-leaved Crowfoot	*Ranunculus sceleratus*

Lesser Celandine	*Ranunculus ficaria*
Water Crowfoot	*Ranunculus aquatilis*
Common Red Poppy	*Papaver rhoeas*
Elm	*Ulmus procera*
Wych Elm	*Ulmus glabra*
Hop	*Humulus lupulus*
Common Nettle	*Urtica dioica*
Pedunculate Oak	*Quercus robur*
Evergreen Oak	*Quercus ilex*
Sweet Chestnut	*Castanea sativa*
Beech	*Fagus sylvatica*
Silver Birch	*Betula pendula*
Alder	*Alnus glutinosa*
Hornbeam	*Carpinus betulus*
Hazel	*Corylus avellana*
Many-seeded Goosefoot	*Chenopodium polyspermum*
Fat Hen	*Chenopodium album*
Chickweed	*Stellaria media*
?Lesser Stitchwort	*Stellaria graminea*?
Greater Stitchwort	*Stellaria holostea*
Ragged Robin	*Lychnis flos-cuculi*
White Campion	*Silene alba*
Red Campion	*Silene dioica*
Redshank	*Persicaria maculosa*
Pale Persicaria	*Persicaria lapathifolia*
Water Pepper	*Persicaria hydropiper*
Knotgrass	*Polygonum aviculare*
Japanese Knotweed	*Fallopia japonica* (possibly now extinct in Newnham)
Black Bindweed	*Fallopia convolvulus*
Sheep's Sorrel	*Rumex acetosella*
Curled Dock	*Rumex crispus*
?Slender St John's-wort	*Hypericum pulchrum*?
Musk Mallow	*Malva moschata*
Lime	*Tilia x vulgaris*

?Woodland Violet	*Viola reichenbachiana*?
Wild Pansy	*Viola tricolor*
Field Pansy	*Viola arvensis*
White Bryony	*Bryonia cretica*
White Poplar	*Populus alba*
Aspen	*Populus tremula*
Lombardy Poplar	*Populus nigra 'Italica'*
?Crack Willow	*Salix fragilis*?
Common Sallow	*Salix cinerea*
Hedge Mustard	*Sisymbrium officinale*
Garlic Mustard	*Alliaria petiolata*
Watercress	*Nasturtium aquaticum*
Cuckoo Flower, Lady's Smock	*Cardamine pratensis*
Shepherd's Purse	*Capsella bursa-pastoris*
Field Pennycress	*Thlaspi arvense*
Rape	*Brassica napus* (not oil seed rape)
Charlock	*Sinapis arvensis*
Primrose	*Primula vulgaris*
Cowslip	*Primula veris*
Yellow Pimpernel	*Lysimachia nemorum*
Yellow Loosestrife	*Lysimachia vulgaris*
Scarlet Pimpernel	*Anagallis arvensis*
Red Currant	*Ribes rubrum*
Meadow Sweet	*Filipendula ulmaria*
Raspberry	*Rubus idaeus*
Bramble, Blackberry	*Rubus fruticosus*
Silverweed	*Potentilla anserine*
Creeping Cinquefoil	*Potentilla reptans*
Barren Strawberry	*Potentilla sterilis*?
Wild Strawberry	*Fragaria vesca*
Wood Avens	*Geum urbanum*
Common Agrimony	*Agrimonia eupatoria*
Dog Rose	*Rosa canina*
Blackthorn, Sloe	*Prunus spinosa*
Bullace	*Prunus domestica insititia*

Crab Apple	*Malus sylvestris*
Rowan	*Sorbus aucuparia*
Whitebeam	*Sorbus aria*
Common Hawthorn	*Crataegus monogyna*
Bird's Foot Trefoil	*Lotus corniculatus*
Greater Bird's Foot Trefoil	*Lotus pedunculatus*
?Common Vetch	*Vicia sativa*?
Tufted Vetch	*Vicia cracca*
Bush Vetch	*Vicia sepium*
Meadow Vetchling	*Lathyrus pratensis*?
White Clover	*Trifolium repens*
Red Clover	*Trifolium pratense*
Common Gorse	*Ulex europaeus*
Great Willow Herb	*Epilobium hirsutum*
Hoary Willow Herb	*Epilobium parviflorum*
Pale Willow Herb	*Epilobium roseum*
Rosebay Willow Herb	*Epilobium angustifolium*
Dogwood	*Cornus sanguinea*
Mistletoe	*Viscum album*
Spindle	*Euonymus europaeus*
Holly	*Ilex aquifolium*
Ivy	*Hedera helix*
Dog's Mercury	*Mercurialis perennis*
?Sun Spurge	*Euphorbia helioscopia*?
Horse Chestnut	*Aesculus hippocastanum*
Common Maple, Hedge Maple	*Acer campestre*
Sycamore	*Acer pseudoplatanus*
Wood Sorrel	*Oxalis acetosella*
Dove's-foot Crane's-bill	*Geranium molle*
Herb Robert	*Geranium robertianum*
Indian Balsam	*Impatiens glandulifera*
Cow Parsley	*Anthriscus sylvestris*
Pignut	*Conopodium majus*
Fool's Parsley	*Aethusa cynapium*
Ground Elder	*Aegopodium podagraria*

Fool's Watercress	*Apium nodiflorum*
?Cowbane	*Cicuta virosa*? (Reportedly killed livestock on Manor Farm land near the Lyde about 1995.)
Hogweed	*Heracleum sphondylium*
Wild Carrot	*Daucus carota*
Common Centaury	*Centaurium erythraea*
Woody Nightshade	*Solanum dulcamara*
Black Nightshade	*Solanum nigrum*
Field Bindweed	*Convolvulus arvensis*
Bindweed	*Calystegia sepium*
Forget-me-not	*Myosotis arvensis*
White Dead-nettle	*Lamium album*
Purple Dead-nettle, Red Dead-nettle	*Lamium purpureum*
Bugle	*Ajuga reptans*
Ground Ivy	*Glechoma hederacea*
Corn Mint	*Mentha arvensis*
Great Plantain	*Plantago major*
Ribwort Plantain	*Plantago lanceolata*
Buddleia	*Buddleja davidii*
Privet	*Ligustrum ovalifolium*
Ash	*Fraxinus excelsior*
Great Mullein	*Verbascum thapsus*
Foxglove	*Digitalis purpurea*
Common Toadflax	*Linaria vulgaris*
Germander Speedwell	*Veronica chamaedrys*
Red Bartsia	*Odontites vernus*
Lady's Bedstraw	*Galium verum*
Goosegrass, Cleavers, ('Sticky')	*Galium aparine*
Moschatel, Townhall Clock	*Adoxa moschatellina*
Elder	*Sambucus nigra*
Wayfaring Tree	*Viburnum lantana*
Honeysuckle	*Lonicera periclymenum*
Common Valerian	*Valeriana officinalis*
Common Teasel	*Dipsacus fullonum*

Small Teasel	*Dipsacus pilosus*
Field Scabious	*Knautia arvensis*
Spear Thistle	*Cirsium vulgare*
Marsh Thistle	*Cirsium palustre*
Creeping Thistle	*Cirsium arvense*
Knapweed	*Centaurea nigra*
Nipplewort	*Lapsana communis*
?Common Cat's Ear	*Hypochoeris radicata*?
Common Hawkbit	*Leontodon taraxacoides*
Common Sowthistle	*Sonchus oleraceus*
Prickly Sow-thistle	*Sonchus asper*
Fox and cubs	*Pilosella aurantiaca*
Dandelion	*Taraxacum officinale*
Fleabane	*Pulicaria dysenterica*
Daisy	*Bellis perennis*
Yarrow	*Achillea millefolium*
Sneezewort	*Achillea ptarmica* (Located in 1989 in the Strings.)
Oxeye Daisy	*Chrysanthemum leucanthemum*
Pineapple-weed	*Matricaria matricarioides*
Scentless Mayweed	*Tripleurospermum inodorum*
Stinking Mayweed	*Anthemis cotula*
Ragwort	*Senecio jacobaea*
?Oxford Ragwort	*Senecio squalidus*?
Groundsel	*Senecio vulgaris*
Coltsfoot	*Tussilago farfara*
Hemp Acrimony	*Eupatorium cannabinum*
Arum Lily, Lords and Ladies	*Arum maculatum*
?Common Duckweed	*Lemna minor*?

Rushes, Sedges & Grasses

Rush various	*Juncus spp.*
Pendulous Sedge	*Carex pendula*
Creeping Fescue	*Festuca rubra*
Rye Grass	*Lolium perenne*

Annual Meadow-grass	*Poa annua*
Smooth Meadow-grass	*Poa pratensis*
Cock's Foot	*Dactylis glomerata*
Wood Melick	*Melica uniflora*
False Oat grass	*Arrhenatherum elatius*
Wild Oat	*Avena fatua*
Winter Wild Oat	*Avena sterilis*
Yorkshire Fog	*Holcus lanatus*
Soft Fog	*Holcus mollis*
Creeping Bent	*Agrostis stolonifera*
Timothy	*Phleum pratense*
Soft Brome	*Bromus hordeaceus*
Couch Grass	*Elymus repens*
Cock's Spur	*Echinochloa crus-galli*
Bulrush, Reed Mace	*Typha latifolia*
Liliaceae	
Solomon's Seal	*Polygonatum multiflorum*
Bluebell	*Hyacinthoides non-scripta*
Tenby Daffodil	*Narcissus pseudonarcissus obvallaris*
Black Bryony	*Tamus communis*
?Broad-leafed Helleborine	*Epipactis helleborine*?
Pyramidal Orchid	*Anacamptis pyramidalis*
Spotted Orchid	*Dactylorhiza fuchsii* (Seems to prefer poor quality land.)
Liverworts	*Bryophyta Sp. indet.* (Frequent along ditches.)
Lichens	(There are several different kinds in Newnham churchyard, also on house roofs and on tree trunks round the village.)

I hope the list will be augmented by others, with more botanical knowledge.

Wildlife In Newnham (2)

Newnham Bird List

My bird records have, on a day-to-day basis, been based on observations on the 25 or so acres of Newnham Hill and Ashmead land, where I have been fortunate enough to wander at will. They are far from complete, but they stretch back to 1943–44 with breaks for time away during National Service, at university and overseas postings. The following attempts to record the birds known to have been in Newnham during the twentieth and early twenty-first centuries, with some idea of their changed status. In square brackets are given the dates when some of the species were first positively identified; these data may help to indicate either a bird's infrequency or how a bird's range is increasing.

Grey Heron	Visitor to garden and other ponds; regularly over flies perhaps to Loddon/Lyde or Andwell Priory Farm fields where many are often to be seen.
Little Egret	[05.08.2004]. Occurs along Loddon (1–3 pairs) and may visit Lyde. Also known on the Whitewater east of Hook.
Mallard	Frequent visitor to ponds and along the Lyde.
Teal	[13.04.2002]. Probably more common than this record suggests.
Shoveler	[03.09.1989].
Canada Goose	Commonly seen over flying and visits the new large pond in Manor Farm's fields.
Mute Swan	January 1948 landed on pond at Newnham Hill. Very infrequent over flyer.
Buzzard	[19.04.1947]. Originally rare but a recent success story. They were scarce until 1996 when they began to be seen more regularly and it is likely that a pair bred in 2000 in Manor Farm woodland, and each year since. In 2005 a pair nested in a spinney at Newnham Hill and another pair is thought to have nested in a spinney between Tylney Lane and Ridge Lane.
Sparrow Hawk	Few but fairly often seen, especially as a bird-table predator.

Red Kite	[20.07.2004]. Subsequently they have increased locally and are seen daily.
Osprey	[01.10.2000]. Single bird on southerly migration.
Hobby	[11.05.1988]. Very rarely seen. May have bred somewhere north of Hook. Reduced numbers of house martins and swallows around Newnham may have made hunting here less productive.
Kestrel	Regularly seen. Sometimes several appear when large silage bales are moved as mice seem to hide under such bales.
Red-legged Partridge	Formerly (WW2 and immediately post-war) rare. A fairly large covey adopted the village about 1990 but the birds were predated.
Grey Partridge	In the 1940s, it was a fairly common breeding species locally. They were around in the second half of the 1960s. But I have no record of them during the past 20 years.
Pheasant	A frequent visitor, probably from some neighbouring shoots.
Corncrake	[Reportedly until 1927].
Moorhen	Found on larger ponds. But has become much less frequent.
Lapwing	Nested at Newnham Hill in 1943; used to nest regularly at Owens Farm, just over the Parish boundary with Hook until about 1985.
Golden Plover	Flying over, but very rarely seen. A flock of ±350 settled at Hale Farm, with Lapwings, in December 2000 for a few days but moved on. Also small flocks may very occasionally be seen over flying in winter.
Snipe	Irregular winter visitor when fields are flooded. Perhaps more frequent along the Lyde.
Woodcock	Used sometimes to be found in brassicas in Newnham Hill kitchen garden. *Possibly* a regular in Manor Farm woods.
Curlew	Very occasional over flyer.
Lesser Black-backed Gull	Fairly regularly seen over flying.
Herring Gull	Fairly regular over flyer.
Common Gull	Very occasionally seen over flying.

Black-headed Gull	Fairly regularly seen in loose groups of up to 100.
Stock Dove	Always few since 1940s and remains uncommon. Perhaps 2–3 pairs breed in the parish in most years.
Wood Pigeon	Common breeding bird and abundant in winter when incomers swell the local population. Regular feeder on acorns, beech mast, ivy berries and haws as well as oilseed rape and clover.
Turtle Dove	Relatively uncommon in 1940s; until 1968 was often encountered; but probably lost as a breeding bird during 1970s. Neither seen nor heard here for two decades or more.
Collared Dove	[Originally noted January 1970.] A common breeding garden bird, often feeding under bird-tables.
Cuckoo	Still heard and seen each year but now becoming rare. More frequent at the northern end of the village.
Barn Owl	In the rather distant past occasional birds were to be seen around the village; nowadays they are probably seldom found at any distance from the Loddon/Lyde valley. A pair has been breeding in a nesting box at the north-west edge of the village.
Little Owl	Used to breed at Newnham Hill until the storm of October 1987 blew down its nest tree. It was not around for some years but in 2002–04 a pair raised young somewhere on Manor Farm land. They may return in the future.
Tawny Owl	Formerly commonly heard.
Swift	About four pairs used to breed in the church. After the nave was re-roofed it became, apparently, inaccessible to the birds and there seems to be only a single pair at present accessing the building at the chancel. In autumn 1999 a swift nesting box was placed under the eaves but it seems not to have been used.
Kingfisher	Present along the Lyde and occasional visitor to garden ponds.
Green Woodpecker	Regularly seen on lawns feeding on ants and thought to breed locally. Most years there is a young bird with one or more adults.

Greater Spotted Woodpecker	A regular bird-table visitor and can be heard drumming in spring. Sometimes they try to access nesting boxes put up for starlings and tits.
Lesser Spotted Woodpecker	[17.09.1943]. Either very rare or seriously overlooked. One was found dazed after colliding with a car in autumn 2004 and thought to have been this species.
Wryneck	[26.06.1950]; used to nest at Newnham Edge until early 1950s.
Sky Lark	Formerly bred. Believed no longer a Newnham resident.
Swallow	Declining numbers because of reduced fly and other insect numbers.
House Martin	Declining numbers because of reduced fly and other insect numbers. There were about 40 nests in the village in the 1990s; currently probably none.
Golden Oriole	[08.06.1976] at the Barracks, Newnham, in early morning, on passage.
Carrion Crow	Regularly seen in small family groups. Breeds within the parish.
Rook	I believe there was a rookery in the 1940s in the small copse about 200 yards north of Lyde Mill beside the Lyde. It exists no longer. Rooks used to visit fields in the parish frequently in the past but they are far less common than before. They often associate with jackdaws, but the latter seem to thrive while rooks have declined.
Jackdaw	Common. Breeds under Kings Bridge and attempts to nest in chimneys in the village and also under the eaves in the church. A species that has done well during the past two or three decades.
Magpie	A fairly common resident breeder.
Jay	Few but regularly breeds.
Great Tit	One of the commonest species in gardens (especially at feeders) and in woodland.
Blue Tit	Probably as common as the Great Tit and found widely.
Coal Tit	Undoubtedly less common than either of the foregoing tits, but a regular visitor to feeders.

Marsh Tit	Rarely seen but sometimes visits feeders.
Willow Tit	Very rarely seen but occasionally visits feeders.
Long-tailed Tit	A fairly regularly observed bird almost anywhere and particularly noticeable when family parties move about in autumn and winter. Predated nests are unfortunately to be found in spring; probably due to carrion crow or magpie destruction, but grey squirrels can also be responsible. Parties sometimes adopt bird-feeders for a while in winter but then move elsewhere. On feeders they can hold their own against seemingly larger birds.
Nuthatch	Regularly seen throughout the year and the song is heard daily in spring. Great patron of feeders in winter.
Treecreeper	Never common but there are probably more than are noted. Can be seen in all months.
Wren	Common in all habitats and heard singing in most months, particularly if surprised. Probably many are overlooked because they scuttle about in thick undergrowth.
Mistle Thrush	Birds with fairly large territories in spring and perhaps because the numbers are fewer than in the past they seem to sing less than formerly. This suggestion is based on the supposition that if territorial males are not threatened by others close by, they have less need to sing.
Fieldfare	Flocks of varying size or even singletons visit each winter, coming and going as it suits them, and feed on berries and fallen apples, and in late winter or spring they feed in the fields, probably on earthworms. Much less common recently due to mild winters on the Continent.
Song Thrush	Although fewer than in the past, these birds have never disappeared from Newnham. Even if not regularly seen, their song can be heard each spring and they are around in autumn and winter but being rather shy they may not be readily seen.
Redwing	The situation is very much as with fieldfares except single birds seem not to be around, and they often mix with fieldfares and groups of other thrushes. Starlings may attach themselves to these winter migrant flocks.

Blackbird	These are regularly in gardens, fields (mostly near hedges) and woodland with good under-storey. And because they are so distinctive and often fairly tame, they are readily seen (in contrast, perhaps, to song thrushes and mistle thrushes). Undoubtedly they are the best songsters hereabouts.
Wheatear	[02.05.1989].
Redstart	[28.08.1989].
Nightingale	Early twentieth century evidently common; still frequent in late 1960s and early 1970s; transient by 1987 and 1988; last noted 25.04.1993.
Robin	Like the blackbird, these are found everywhere and are more trusting of people than most other birds. (Treecreepers and goldcrests are, in my experience, as trusting or possibly more so; perhaps because they are so small and insignificant they are seldom seen and never persecuted.) They sing with varying frequency in every month, but their winter air is a pale, sad warble in comparison with their spring and summer aggressive, territorial song.
Grasshopper Warbler	Always rare; last heard about 1980.
Sedge Warbler	[16.08.1943], may be regular by the Lyde.
Blackcap	Becoming less common.
Garden Warbler	Becoming less common.
Whitethroat	Now very uncommon.
Lesser Whitethroat	Probably only transient now.
Willow Warbler	Now an irregular visitor.
Chiffchaff	Now much less common than formerly.
Goldcrest	Uncommon but probably overlooked.
Firecrest	Has been reported from the northern end of the village.
Spotted Flycatcher	Formerly nesting in very many Newnham gardens, now rare.
Pied Flycatcher	[25.08.1984]: presumably an autumn migrant.
Dunnock	Regular but declining species.
Meadow pipit	Probably used to breed, now very occasionally seen in winter.

Pied Wagtail	A very few breed around the village.
White Wagtail	Seen once in winter.
Grey Wagtail	Believed to breed at Lyde Mill, has bred near bottom of Crown Lane and at Newnham Hill (once).
Yellow Wagtail	[25.08.1990]; but may breed on the Lyde.
Starling	Much less common than formerly but may be increasing. There used to be very large flocks (several hundred birds) in autumn/winter when the rubbish tip below the bridge in Crown Lane still operated.
Hawfinch	[26.04.1946] and once or twice since; probably overlooked.
Greenfinch	Has become very uncommon.
Goldfinch	Much less common than in the past.
Siskin	[28.03.1989]; subsequently at bird-table most winters.
Linnet	Formerly frequent breeder; rare since about 1995.
Redpoll	[05.03.2004] on bird-feeder (with siskins).
Bullfinch	Always uncommon, now very infrequently seen or heard.
Chaffinch	Formerly very common but has declined in recent years.
Brambling	Infrequent visitor during winter.
Yellowhammer	Formerly frequently seen/heard, now uncommon or rare probably due to lack of wheat and barley crops around the village.
House Sparrow	During and before 1940s (perhaps 1950s) a very common resident, now about two breeding pairs in the village.

Wildlife In Newnham (3)

Mammals

Hedgehog	*Erinaceus europaeus*	Common
Pygmy Shrew	*Sorex minutus*	Probably common. Comes into houses.
Mole	*Talpa europaea*	Common, in some years very active.
Common Pipistrelle 45*	*Pipistrellus pipistrellus*	Echolocates at 45 kHz.
Soprano Pipistrelle 55*	*Pipistrellus pygmaeus*	Echolocates at 55 kHz.
Brown Long-eared Bat*	*Plecotus auritus*	
Serotine*	*Eptesicus serotinus*	
Noctule*	*Nyctalus noctula*	
Rabbit	*Oryctolagus cuniculus*	Abundant but frequently suffers myxomatosis.
Brown Hare	*Lepus europaeus*	Very uncommon near the village, some found near the Lyde.
Red Squirrel	*Sciurus vulgaris*	Last seen (by me) about 1938 at Newnham Hill.
Grey Squirrel	*Neosciurus carolinensis*	Abundant and a major pest.
Dormouse	*Muscardinus avellanarius*	Believed to be present but very rare.
Short-tailed Vole	*Microtus agrestis*	Possibly this species.
Harvest Mouse	*Micromys minutus*	Formerly present when cereals grown locally.
Yellow-necked Mouse	*Apodemus flavicollis*	Some are certainly present.
Brown Rat	*Rattus norvegicus*	Common – abundant and a major pest.
House Mouse	*Mus musculus*	Common – abundant and a major pest.
Red Fox	*Vulpes vulpes*	Common and very damaging to domestic poultry.
Badger	*Meles meles*	Uncommon but present. May still breed in Compfield Copse.

Stoat	*Mustela erminea*	Seldom seen but present in small numbers.
Weasel	*Mustela nivalis*	Seldom seen but present in small numbers.
Muntjac	*Muntiacus reevesi*	First seen here about 1985, undoubtedly increasing in numbers.
Roe Deer	*Capreolus capreolus*	Common and very damaging in gardens.

* On 13 June 2004, Naomi Ewald, of Hampshire Wildlife Trust, brought a bat identification device and we walked all round the village, including down almost to Hill Copse, and these were the species found.

Wildlife In Newnham (4)

Newnham Butterfly List

Essex Skipper	This or Small Skipper are often seen but not in every year. These are difficult to separate in the field, both occur.
Small Skipper	(see above)
Large White	Abundant before and during the 1940s, in decline since; now relatively uncommon.
Small White	Formerly abundant, now few.
Green-veined White	Formerly common, now much fewer.
Orange Tip	Seldom on the wing before or after May.
Clouded Yellow	During 1943 or 1944, there were major incursions; subsequently I have seen one only once, on 25.08.2000.
Pale Clouded Yellow	In 1943 or 1944, a very rare visitor.
Brimstone	Never common, but regularly found from March to September.
Purple Emperor	Wing of one found in Newnham Hill about 1982. No living specimen seen.
White Admiral	Rare visitor.
Small Tortoiseshell	Fairly common in most years; far fewer recently.
Comma	Never common, usually only singles.
Painted Lady	Most years, a few appear; sometimes in considerable numbers.
Red Admiral	Some hibernated adults appear early spring, but their main season seems to be when the asters are flowering and then when orchard fruit are well ripened. Some years they are plentiful. Can sometimes be seen in October flying south – evidently some Red Admirals migrate.
Peacock	A declining species.
Silver Washed Fritillary	Very rare.
Marbled White	Very occasional visitor, presumably from chalk areas to the south.
Meadow Brown	Probably now our commonest butterfly between mid-June and mid-August.

Gatekeeper	Common in appropriate habitat, July to mid-August.
Small Heath	Formerly fairly readily found here; in recent years, very rare.
Speckled Wood	Regularly in woodland glades.
Wall Brown	During 1940s it could be found regularly in Newnham; not seen here for a very long time.
Small Copper	Formerly, this species was regularly found here, but is seldom seen nowadays.
Holly Blue	Few every year.
Common Blue	Less common than the above, but found in most years.

I suspect that Ringlets also occur, but have been missed or confused with other 'browns'. It is also likely that Purple Hair Streaks can be found high in Newnham's oak trees.

APPENDIX 4

Wildlife In Newnham (5)

Other Fauna in Newnham

Amphibians		
Smooth Newt	*Triturus vulgaris*	Present in most ponds for part of the year.
Crested Newt	*Triturus cristatus*	*ditto*
Palmate Newt	*Triturus helveticus*	*ditto*
Common Toad	*Bufo bufo*	Small numbers found in most gardens.
Common Frog	*Rana temporaria*	Less commonly found than formerly in all ponds.
Reptiles		
Slow-worm	*Anguis fragilis*	Not often seen, probably more common than supposed.
Viviparous Lizard	*Zootoca vivipara*	Probably this species used to be found basking in summer sun on walls etc. Not seen for years.
Grass Snake	*Natrix natrix*	Seldom seen but probably not uncommon.
Adder	*Vipera berus*	Very seldom seen.
Wasps		
Hornet	*Vespa crabro*	Few but seemingly becoming more common.
Common Wasp*	*Vespula vulgaris*	Common (underground nester).
German Wasp*	*Vespula germanica*	Common (house roof nester).
Tree Wasp*	*Dolichovespula norwegica*	Uncommon (hedgerow nester).

* Assuming the nesting sites are sufficiently diagnostic all three species can be found here.

Bumble Bees

At least two species are regularly found and these may be *Bombus terrestris* and *Bombus lapidarius.*

Coleoptera

June bug (Cockchafer)	*Melolontha melolontha*	Now a rarely seen insect, sometimes attracted into houses by electric light.
Glow-worm	*Lampyris noctiluca*	A very seldom-found visitor.

Odonata

Beautiful Demoiselle	*Calopteryx virgo*	Sometimes visits.
Red Damselfly (?Large Red Damselfly)	*Pyrrhosoma nymphula*	Regularly seen.
?Common Blue Damselfly	*Enallagma cyathigerum*	Regularly seen.
?Azure Damselfly	*Coenagrion puella*	*ditto*
Broad-bodied Chaser	*Libellula depressa*	Sometimes visits.

Molluscs

Garden Snail	*Helix aspersa*	Pest for gardeners, much favoured by song thrushes.